The Center
for the Advancement of
Teaching and Learning

*SELECTED PAPERS*
*from the*
*16th INTERNATIONAL CONFERENCE*
*on*
*COLLEGE TEACHING*
*AND LEARNING*

Edited by
Jack A. Chambers

*Florida Community College*
*at Jacksonville*

ISBN 1-931997-03-9

Center for the Advancement of Teaching and Learning, *Florida Community College at Jacksonville*, 501 W. State Street, Room 441, Jacksonville, FL 32202.

# CONTENTS

Foreword                           vi.

**A Step Too Far? Are We Abusing
the Concept of Left Brain/Right Brain
in Learning and Development?**          1
     Julia Claxton
     *York St. John College, UK*

**Electronic Portfolios: High-Stake
Assessments in Graduate Level
Distance Education Programs**          21
     Joseph-Rene Corbeil
     Cheng-Chang Pan
     Michael J. Sullivan
     *University of Texas at Brownsville*
     and *Texas Southmost College*

**Integrating Business Ethics into an
Undergraduate Business Curriculum**          35
     David B. Dahlberg
     Gregory B. DiNovis
     *College of St. Catherine*

**E-Learning Options and
the Challenges of Change**          45
      Jeana M. Davis
      *Florida Community College
      at Jacksonville*


**Teaching for Learning in the
Community College: Integrating
the Scholarship of Teaching and
Learning, Information Literacy
and Technology**          81
      Ruby Evans
      *University of Central Florida*


**The Interactive Art of Critical Thinking**    97
      Barclay Hudson
      *Fielding Graduate Institute*


**A Blended Course on Feature Writing
For Newspapers and Magazines**          121
      Yanick Rice Lamb
      *Howard University*


**Instructor Personalities and
Teaching with Computers**          131
      Claire Rundle
      *Regent University*

**Teaching Activity-Based Introductory Physics
In Large Classes: The SCALE-UP Project**     **141**
Jeffery M. Saul
*University of Central Florida*
Robert J. Beichner
*North Carolina State University*


**Individualism, Community
And Academic Integrity**     **171**
Nancy A. Stanlick
*University of Central Florida*


**Integrating Learning, Reflective E-Portfolios,
Undergraduate Research and Assessment**     **185**
Benjamin R. Stephens
Barbara E. Weaver
*Clemson University*


**Learning a la Mode de Paris**     **203**
Katherine Watson
*Coastline Community College*


**Contributors**     **211**

# FOREWORD

The Center for the Advancement of Teaching and Learning (CATL) was developed in 1987 when Florida Community College at Jacksonville accepted K. Patricia Cross' challenge to use the classroom as a modern laboratory for conducting experiments to gauge the impact of teaching on student learning.

The philosophy of the Center for the Advancement of Teaching and Learning is that classroom teachers are the key to improving student learning; the Center is therefore composed of faculty members under the guidance of a steering committee which consists of faculty from each of the four major campuses of the College. Part of the Center's success can be attributed to the numerous opportunities given to faculty to test their teaching ideas and to put research results into practice.

Center Steering Committee members serve as Campus Mentors and as sponsors of faculty development programs, both college-wide and on each campus. The Center also supports faculty mini-grants for classroom research and professional development and sponsors a number of awards honoring teaching faculty. The Center itself has been the recipient of an award—the Theodore M. Hesburgh Certificate of Excellence—for its faculty development programs. In an effort to stimulate creative discussion and promote experimentation to improve the teaching/learning process, as well as to honor those who have already significantly improved learning in higher education, the Center annually sponsors an international conference. The conference features recognized educational leaders in diverse areas of teaching, learning and technology. Since its inception, the conference has grown steadily and now attracts nearly 1,000 scholars annually from around the world. This publication, *Selected Papers*, was created as a result of Center interest in honoring faculty who develop some of the most outstanding contributions to the conference. It also preserves and makes available the contributions made to the teaching profession as a whole. *Selected Papers* is covered online by the American Psychological Association's PsycINFO.

Many people are responsible for the success of the annual conference. We would like to thank all participants, including featured speakers and workshop leaders; presenters from universities, liberal arts and community colleges throughout the United States and abroad; faithful attendees; and Florida Community College faculty and staff who give so generously of their time and efforts each year to help the conference continue its success.

Both the international conference and the *Selected Papers* journal have increased in growth and focus over the years. This year's publication contains articles selected as the 12 best papers of those submitted to the *Sixteenth International Conference on College Teaching and Learning;* they represent a cross-section of nearly 300 faculty presentations. All papers submitted for consideration in this year's journal were reviewed by the Florida Community College faculty members listed below. Papers were judged on the following criteria:

- Quality of content

- Quality of writing and presentation

vii

- Focus of the paper (i.e., teaching, learning, technology)

- Discipline

- Appeal to an audience of professional, post-secondary educators

- Theoretical or practical applications

We hope you will find the ideas presented here applicable and inspirational to your own teaching, learning and research. Please plan to join us at the *Seventeenth International Conference on College Teaching and Learning*, April 10-14. 2006, in Jacksonville, Florida.

Victoria M. McGlone     Jeffrey T. Olma
Librarian     Professor of English

John Q. Mullins     Courtney S. Summerlin
Professor of Biology     Professor of Legal Studies

Ronald S. Wolf
Professor of Culinary Arts

# A STEP TOO FAR?

# ARE WE ABUSING THE CONCEPT OF

# LEFT BRAIN/ RIGHT BRAIN

# IN LEARNING AND DEVELOPMENT?

**Julia Claxton**
*York St John College, UK*

## INTRODUCTION

The purpose of this paper is to highlight the dangers of the concept of being "right brained or left brained" in learning and teaching. It provides a multidisciplinary approach drawing from literature in neuroscience and psychology and relates this to learning and teaching. It seeks to identify the false assumptions that comprise a paradigm leap that is being used today in tools used for learning development which communicate the right brained or left brained concept to learners. The paper aims to illustrate the types of errors made and what their effect can be to the learner. It suggests a more positive way forward for exploring diversity of thinking amongst learners.

Learning styles, thinking styles, personality indicators, etc. are there to help people to understand themselves and to understand others, and in particular, to appreciate the "richness" that comes from diversity. However, there is a darker side to this type of categorization (see Figure 1).

1

**Figure 1**
**Paradigm Leap in use of "Right Brained**
**or Left Brained" Concept**

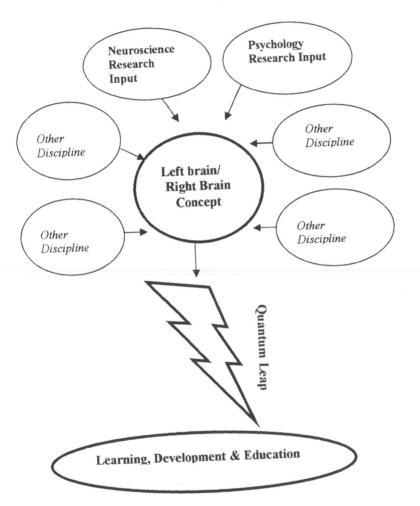

# RESEARCH
# ON RIGHT BRAINED/LEFT BRAINED CONCEPT

The right brained/left brained concept is used in numerous development programs and more recently in the school and college classroom. This is interesting, but on examination of some of the assumptions, explanations and techniques being used—and in particular on examination of some of the tools which seek to determine whether individuals are so-called right brained or left-brained—the picture becomes somewhat worrisome. The reason for concern is that when compared to the actual literature and research that has been carried out, many of the materials that are being used in the learning and development programs often evidence a massive paradigm leap from fact into fantasy. This can result in persons being given unreliable information and thus misled.

## The Human Brain

The human brain is made of two hemispheres which are joined together by a communicating fibre. In a normal person the two sides communicate with each other. However, the two sides have been shown to support particular thinking processes in different ways. This has been shown particularly in people in which the communicating fiber has been cut or where there has been brain damage on one side of the brain. In such cases individuals find they cannot complete certain physical or mental tasks. Concerning physical motor tasks this is shown clearly in tests where one side of the brain is anaesthetised. Shortly after the anaesthetic is administered to one side of the brain the individual loses the use of the opposite side of their body to that which was given the anaesthetic.

Concerning mental tasks, experiments on split-brain patients (Springer & Deutsch,1981)—i.e., patients who have had the communication fiber cut so that the two sides of the brain cannot communicate with each other)—have shown that while an individual recognizes an object which has been shown to the right hemisphere only, the individual cannot find the word to describe what it is because the right brain cannot tell the left brain what it is.

## Specialization Theory

Experiments of this kind led to the theory of "specialization" of tasks of each side of the brain—that there are some tasks in which one side of the brain specializes. EEG scans also confirm that different activities cause activity in different parts of the brain. However, and it is an important however, it does not seem possible to talk about specialization in this sense since thought processes are so complex. Hellige (1993) points this out very clearly in his writings.

Even when it has been ascertained biologically that one hemisphere supports a particular thinking process, because that process is lost or impaired when damage occurs to that hemisphere, it does not mean that the hemisphere specializes in that thinking process. Vitally supporting a thinking process, somewhere along its path, does not mean that the hemisphere completes the process on its own or even that it completes most of the process—a small chink can break the chain. Herein lies the unstable foundation of many of the assumptions of the right brain/left brain concept—the unstable foundation of specialization.

If the foundation of specialization is accepted then the following assumptions follow:

- The first assumption here is that there is indeed an associated list of thinking skills for each hemisphere. That is, that one hemisphere has one set of complete thinking processes and the other has a different set and that these can be identified for each. Many people can identify with these and many will talk in the left brain/right brain language. Thinking processes such as logical, sequential and linear are often attributed to the left brain while creativity, intuition and perception are often attributed to the right hemisphere. As research progresses it is showing this attribution is not accurate and that thinking processes are so complex that to break them down into their parts for testing becomes almost meaningless

- The second assumption is that if an individual has some of the thinking skills associated with that hemisphere that they should also have a natural tendency for the others attributed to that same hemisphere. Therefore, if someone is shown to be logical they are probably good sequential thinkers too because both these are often associated to the left brain. Conversely, if someone is shown to be intuitive, there may be the assumption that they must also be creative as both are associated with the right brain

- The third assumption is that if they show a tendency for a number of the processes in one hemisphere that they are unlikely to be strong in those associated with the other hemisphere. That is, if someone is logical then they are probably not intuitive, since this is attributed to the right hemisphere. These three assumptions alone, if accepted, could be very damaging to learning and teaching

***Origin of Specialization Theory.*** Along with the above there is a need to consider the origin of the specialization concept as this alone highlights a problem with its use. The discovery that the two hemispheres of the brain work in a different way came about through observing people who had had the connecting tissue (corpus collusum) of these two hemispheres severed so that the brain had effectively become two separate processors rather than one whole processor as in normal human brains.

Numerous experiments showed that in patients in which the two hemispheres were separated, there were differences in the processing abilities of the left and right hemisphere. Although comparisons of each hemisphere separately can be made between split-brains and normal brains, normal brains have no restriction on the communication between each hemisphere. Additionally the speed of communication has been shown to be extremely fast. Is the concept of two different sides therefore just an unhelpful illusion?

***Specialization as a Metaphor.*** If the concept of specialization merely becomes a metaphor, as many in learning and teaching use it now—*is the metaphor itself harmful?* It still establishes the grouping and separation that can be so misleading. It still talks of dominance and still talks about linking certain processes together and still talks about separating those two groups from one another. It still promulgates the idea that a left brained person is logical, sequential, numeric, detailed, vertical, and a right brained person intuitive, holistic, creative, musical, lateral, and spatial. The judgement as to whether someone is classified 'left brained' or 'right brained' is determined into which category their thinking strengths, or rather those most easily measured or observed, tend to fall.

One of the main factors that decides whether the grouping can be used positively or negatively is where there is a different value attributed to one group of thinking. Different types of thinking give different approaches to problem solving, decision making, planning, etc., and if these are viewed as left brain or right brain tasks, then an individual could find themselves being valued in a particular way if they have been categorized as a left brain or right brain thinker.

In an enlightened context the value given to particular thinking styles can be challenged, but if you are the only person with strong intuitive thinking and all the others do not have this ability, then your strength could be devalued. On the other hand, if others are aware of all the different types of thinking and know they have a need for diversity, they may welcome in their mind, a more 'right brained' approach. It can also highlight the sheer number of different approaches available and also indicate whether some approaches are lacking or over-empowering some less populated approaches. It can help those who feel they are in minority to label their thinking approach and see it appear in black and white as an identified way of thinking.

## DISCUSSION

It may be helpful to reflect on the fact that the value of a person's thinking is not determined by whether they are in line with the thinking of the majority of people in their group but in the fact that if they are in the minority then they are needed all the more to bring a balance. The notion of a "balance" then brings back the idea of two different approaches, that is, left brain and right brain. Therefore this may be a positive feature of the notion as without it there may not be the desire to have a balance.

This point also leads into discussions concerning whether certain organizations actually recruit only a proportion of the diversity of thinking approaches. In higher education there is more and more emphasis on form filling and procedures which could lead to valuing sequential thinking higher than creative thinking. *In appointing and promoting faculty is there a danger of screening out the more creative thinkers?*

### Effects of 'Specialization Theory' on Students

*What about students? Do recruitment strategies filter out students who do not appear at interviews and on application forms to have those thinking processes the academics can identify as helpful? Could students accuse academics of selecting people on the basis of evidence of certain thinking strengths over others? Are assumptions made concerning the thinking strengths on an individual which is related to grouping certain thinking processes together? Do academics know which thinking skills are most valued in their institution?*

*If a student shows a strong aptitude for creative thinking does this mean they may not be logical?* There is no evidence to suggest this, yet this quantum leap is promulgated in numerous learning and development arenas around the world today.

On an even more dangerous level, if this attitude is exposed to others, and in particular influential others, this can have a profound effect on how a person is viewed. If a student hopes to work with a particular professor on some research but has been categorized as being creative (and therefore not logical) this may affect her/his chances of being selected for the research.

*Does an academic's own personal biases of how s/he values certain thinking processes make the student a victim of discrimination?* This was exactly the problem caused within one organization which sought to improve understanding of diversity by running a seminar on differences in learning styles and looking at four different styles to see which one you were. Months later one attendee reported:

> *I felt as if I had been pigeon-holed and what was most upsetting was that I noticed that since that day people have talked to me differently from what they had been doing before and not asking me to be involved in certain projects anymore. I feel as if I'm now in a certain zone that I've been put in and it's going to take effort for me to get people to see that I'm not in that zone or any zone and that I'm not that limited.*

Sometimes the best intentions do not work and in this case the seminar did not have the benefit of showing strength in diversity as had been planned. Also, another important question is that if others recognize our strengths and then try to play to them is this manipulation? The context in which these ideas are explored is essential. It is easier to abuse the concept if people are not being sufficiently aware of the dangers. People should be told about the possible downside of such exploration and in that knowledge can make their own decision as to whether to attend such seminars.

Understanding the context means identifying the present culture and the readiness of individuals to be able to get positive results from such an experience. It can be a powerful tool to identify strengths and diversity and understanding of different approaches, but in the wrong context it can be a manipulative tool to fast track getting to know people in order to get the best performance out of them. People within organizations need to be really honest and ask some hard questions about motives for these kinds of initiatives. If the culture is already one of allowing, enabling and learning, and is genuinely using coaching, mentoring and listening, then it may well be the right environment to introduce the concepts and they will be useful. However, in a blame culture with a definite preference for certain thinking styles and a greater value put on some of them, then it can be divisive and destructive. Educators and academics need to be careful to consider the context in which they are introducing such concepts.

**Thinking**

It is also essential to know what is meant by the term "thinking." Thinking is complex and to break it down into small enough parts to test out it can become meaningless. For instance, the literature to date broadly supports the notion that "recognizing unfamiliar blurred faces" is something which the right hemisphere can do better than the left hemisphere. Note the exactness of each word here: recognizing, not remembering; unfamiliar, not familiar; blurred, not clear; and faces, not pictures or words. This cannot be generalized into "remembering faces."

Even if it is accepted that the right hemisphere, rather than the left, is better at doing this specific task, it does not necessarily mean that the right is completely responsible for this task. All that can be said is that some vital part of that process resides in the right hemisphere so much so that when it is not involved, the left hemisphere struggles to complete the task well. It may be that by not using the right hemisphere there is a 'chink in the armor' but that some of the armor is still functioning fine and some of it may reside in the left hemisphere. So a whole thinking process or task even for such a carefully "boiled down" or dissected process as the one in this example cannot be attributed purely to the right hemisphere. It can only be said that the right hemisphere does contribute and/or support a vital part of that process. (Hellige,1993).

**Generalization**

An example of misuse of generalization is found in the following question which appears in a learning tool for a management development program used in a large British company: *Do you remember faces easily?* for which a "yes" is attributed to right brain and a "no" to left brain. Early research showed that patients with right brain lesions or split-brained patients could not recognize faces (Hecaen & Angelergues,1962; Milner, 1968) and that in normal brains the faces were perceived more clearly by the right hemisphere (Levy, Trevarthen, & Sperry, 1972; Milner & Dunne 1977; Schwartz & Smith 1980). However as more and more research has been carried out (Bruce, 1982; Hellige, Corwin, & Johnson, 1984; Sergent, 1985; Freeman,1980), the only thing that can really be said now is that the right brain does seem to have the process for recognizing unfamiliar faces.

Familiar faces, however, are a different matter. These have been shown to have different neural pathways than unfamiliar faces; also expression of face is a different pathway (Bruce & Young, 1986). For faces of people personally known there is the complexity of knowing a personality and having a relationship with the person. With a familiar face but unknown person there will be information as to why the face is familiar—perhaps an actor or a famous person or perhaps a name or occupation is known which the left hemisphere can use to help it remember a face.

Recognition of faces also depends on what type of face and whether more than just a face is considered. This is because the left hemisphere can process and store faces but it does it in a different way. It remembers the more local information of nose, eyes, eyebrows—and in particular, noticeable features like hair, beard and glasses—whereas the right brain will process the more holistic overall image and is therefore much better at recognizing a blurred image than the left hemisphere. The latter requires more of the detail to be in focus. Teuber (1978) even stated that face recognition was possible without a right brain at all. Therefore, the question—*Do you remember faces?*—is far too general to determine anything and thus serves as an example of the many generalizations that occur in such learning tools.

*Who Is Responsible?* So who is responsible for ensuring that in learning and development we do not fall into the pitfall of generalization? There is a need to consider the power that a presenter has in any learning setting because students will receive the information with a sense of authority. Therefore, the responsibility must fall mainly to the presenter.

Part of the responsibility is to make sure that all materials are accurate and backed-up by research. However, it is also important to encourage dialogue around the benefits and possible problems with using any tool well before their intended use. The context needs to be understood and handled.

## Accuracy and Words

Another illustration from a learning tool, designed to ascertain whether a person is left brained or right brained, brings to the attention the important of "accuracy" and "words" which are used when this concept is tested. The following is a question in which respondents are asked to select which of the following best describes them "concerning hunches." The options are:

A.  I frequently have strong ones and follow them

B.  I have strong hunches but don't place much faith in them

C.  I occasionally have hunches but don't place much faith in them

D.  I would not rely on hunches to help me make important decisions

The word "hunches" is being used to mean "intuition," which is one of the most difficult thinking processes to research but is frequently reported as relating to the right hemisphere. Therefore, this question does seem to have some research back-up, in terms of a strong sense of intuition could suggest dominance of the right brain.

However, the structure of the questions do not ask whether the person has hunches but whether they *follow* them or not. This brings in a multitude of other factors such as self-esteem, self-confidence, social norms and occupational freedom. Answer "D" would in fact cover the person with strong intuition but who feels they cannot rely on it for important decisions due to low self-confidence and non-acceptance of this thinking process in their work environment. If they were to choose "D" the scoring would classify them as left brain dominant.

Another question asks about handwriting position. This is an interesting attempt to consider handedness, which to be fair, most questionnaires do not include at all. Again however, it is flawed because it is too simplistic.

If there is to be a link made between thinking and handedness then it is important to be more exact about determining someone's handedness. For instance, there are many reasons why people are left handed, some due to hereditary factors, some pathological factors and some chemicals in the mother's blood or womb. It is essential to find out which before a classification of the type of left handedness can even be made. Also, asking people whether they are left handed or not assumes that they actually know. It also assumes they are basing this diagnosis on a particular skill for which they use that hand. Many people use both hands for different tasks and accurate classification in itself is a major task.

**The Conflict**

*So, should academics be using the concept of right brain/left brain to help their students to learn? And, how aware are academics of the value they place on particular learning skills of students. Is there some intrinsic assumed hierarchy?*

There are companies who are putting their staff through right brain/left brain training. The information they are receiving is not supported by research; however, individuals tend to genuinely believe that they now know whether they are right brained or left brained. They now know they should be good at certain things and not good at others. This is turn affects their self-perception on their abilities to carry out certain tasks. Clearly this could limit their development rather than enhance it.

## A BETTER WAY FORWARD

*So is there a better way forward?*   Figure 2 illustrates the components needed to ensure a responsible use of the concept.

**Figure 2**
**Suggested Model for Use of "Right Brained or Left Brained" Concept**

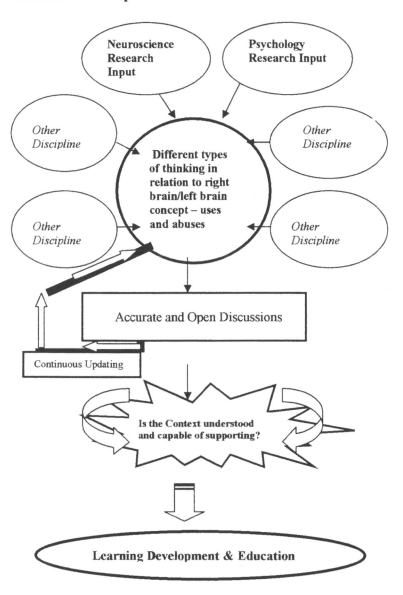

Research clearly shows there are differences in the processing abilities of right and left brains. There are also indicators related to handedness, gender and medical conditions, etc. To deny this is contrary to the evidence and would not be helpful. However, it must be acknowledged that most people have normal brains in which the interconnecting communication tissues are fully intact. Thus, in normal situations (where the attempt is not to deliberately arouse one side of the brain more than the other), individuals can access the thinking processes of both sides of the brain. Of course, persons have individual strengths, but these can relate to a myriad of factors, i.e., personality, upbringing, social conditioning, etc. Some of these can be explored while some are almost impossible to investigate.

In order to allow individuals to explore their full capabilities, perhaps a more open approach may be helpful. A practical suggestion would be to ask a group of students to list all the types of thinking that they can generate. Students therefore focus on "thinking about thinking" and the richness of diversity that exists. This alone is important learning. It brings about an array of thinking types such as logical thinking, sequential thinking, metaphorical thinking, synthesizing, creative thinking, emotional thinking, holistic thinking and detailed thinking, as well as general debate as to what is thinking, anyway.

Depending on the culture and whether people are likely to value different thinking processes more highly that others (which can become destructive), individuals could select processes that they feel are real strengths for them and then talk about whether they use fully these in their studies, and if not, how this might be facilitated. They can talk about thinking approaches they do not tend to use and whether they might want to explore using them more. This approach, while giving labels to thinking processes, does not have any assumptions of linkage and assumed groupings within it.

It is also important to inform students as to the pitfalls of assuming linkages in thinking and to give them as much responsibility as possible over the exercises they are carrying out. The extent to which the discussions should be shared and open depends on the context of the group and whether stereotyping is likely or not. It is essential that the academic knows the context of the group.

## SUMMARY AND CONCLUSIONS

In summary, the metaphor of left brain/right brain thinking has many pitfalls of which the academic and student alike need to be aware. The paradigm leap that is so commonly represented in education today needs to be strongly challenged, lest we rob individuals of their perceived ability to develop in every area of their thinking.

## REFERENCES

Bruce, V. (1982). Changing faces: Visual and non-visual coding processes in face recognition. *British Journal of Psychology, 73,* 105-116

Bruce, V., & Young, A. (1986). Understanding face recognition. *British Journal of Psychology, 77,* 305-327.

Freeman, J. (1980). *Cerebral asymmetries in the processing of faces.* Unpublished doctoral dissertation, University of Aberdeen, Scotland.

Hecaen, H., & Angelergues, R. (1962). Agnosia for faces (prosopagnosia). *Archives of Neurology 7,* 92-100.

Hellige, J. (1993). *Hemispheric asymmetry: What's right and what's left?* Cambridge, MA: Harvard University Press.

Hellige, J., Corwin, W., & Jonssen. J. E. (1984). Effects of perceptual quality on the processing of human faces presented to the left and right cerebral hemispheres. *Journal of Experimental Psychology: Human Perception and Performance, 10,* 90-107

Levy, J., Trevarthen, C., & Sperry, R. (1972). Perception of bilateral chimeric figures following hemispheric deconnection. *Brain, 95,* 61-78.

Milner, A., & Dunne, J. (1977). Lateralized perception of bilateral chimaeric faces by normal subjects. *Nature, London* 268, No 5616, 175-176.

Milner, B. (1968). Visual recognition and recall after right temporal lobe excision in man. *Neuropsychologia, 6,* 191-209.

Schwartz, M., & Smith, M. (1980). Visual asymmetries with chimeric stimuli. *Neuropsychologia, 18,* 103-106.

Sergent, J. (1985). Influence of task and input factors on hemispheric involvement in face processing. *Journal of Experimental Psychology: Human Perception and Performance, 11,* 846-861

Springer, S., & Deutsch, G. (1981). *Left brain: Right brain, perspectives from cognitive neuroscience* (5th ed.). New York: Freeman.

Teuber, H. (1978). The brain and human behaviour. In R. Held, H. W. Leibowitz, & H. L. Teuber (Eds.), *Handbook of sensory physiology* (V. 8). Berlin: Springer-Verlag.

# ELECTRONIC PORTFOLIOS:

# HIGH-STAKES ASSESSMENTS

# IN GRADUATE-LEVEL

# DISTANCE EDUCATION PROGRAMS

**Joseph-Rene Corbeil**
**Cheng-Chang Pan**
**Michael J. Sullivan**
*University of Texas at Brownsville*
and *Texas Southmost College*

## INTRODUCTION

According to a study conducted in 2002 by the American Association of Colleges of Teacher Education (Salzman, Denner, & Harris, 2002), approximately 90 percent of schools, colleges, and departments of education currently use portfolios to make decisions regarding student admission, retention, and promotion. Forty percent use portfolios for teacher certification or licensing. Given the pervasiveness of assessment portfolios in higher education, a need to study the components and effective uses of such tools was indicated in order to assess their value as high-stakes assessment instruments. This paper provides background information and then addresses several major themes: 1) creating and implementing e-portfolio assessments; 2) a generalized model for e-portfolio design; and 3) a list of requirements and caveats for implementing portfolios as an alternative to traditional high-stakes assessments.

21

## BACKGROUND INFORMATION

An e-portfolio is a purposeful collection of work that exhibits the students' efforts, progress, and achievements in digital form. Students create projects or perform tasks on predetermined standards, criteria, and indicators which are evaluated by scoring rubrics. Consensus seems strong within the educational community with regard to the use of portfolios for reinforcing learning and for making formative decisions about candidate knowledge, skills, dispositions, and growth. However, some have strong reservations about using e-portfolios for high-stakes assessment. A thorough understanding of the issues surrounding the use of portfolio assessment requires an appraisal of the potential benefits and risks of this assessment medium.

### Why Use E-Portfolios?

For the past eighteen months, the faculty of the Online Master of Education. in Educational Technology at The University of Texas at Brownsville and Texas Southmost College have been carefully studying the benefits and risks of adopting the e-portfolio as an alternative assessment method to the existing paradigm of the comprehensive examination. Three primary reasons for considering this change have been identified, as listed below.

*Quality   Control.* While   a   comprehensive examination can provide insight into a candidate's readiness for becoming a practitioner in the field, a more authentic assessment is needed than the candidate's ability to produce an essentially academic paper on a word processor. Graduates must be able to demonstrate both a solid familiarity of research in the field, as well as a proven capacity to integrate the latest research findings into practice.

*Logistics.* The candidates of the Online M.Ed. represent a geographically disparate group. Given the rigid standards for proctor qualification and selection, proctoring the comprehensive exam is becoming progressively more cost prohibitive and logistically complicated, particularly when candidates reside in foreign countries or are on active military duty overseas.

*Program Evaluation and Research.* An authentic assessment of student ability may contribute to a more rigorous evaluation of the program. A successful e-portfolio could provide a wealth of data for evaluation of the program itself, students' academic development, changes in effective uses of instructional technologies and a diversity of experiences in the applications of those technologies.

## CREATING AND IMPLEMENTING
## E-PORTFOLIO ASSESSMENTS

Implementing an e-portfolio assessment system can seem overwhelming, but it becomes less arduous if viewed as a series of stages, each with its own goals and activities. Such activities are outlined below.

### Overview

The general steps involved in the e-portfolio creation process can be summarized as follows (Ivers & Barron, 1998):

- **Assess/Decide.** Conduct a needs assessment of the audience, the presentation goals, and the appropriate tools for the final e-portfolio presentation.

- **Design/Plan.** Organize or design the presentation; determine audience-appropriate content, software, storage medium, and presentation sequence and construct flow charts or write storyboards.

- **Develop.** Gather materials to include in the presentation and organize into a sequence (or use hyperlinks) for the best presentation, using an appropriate multimedia authoring program.

- **Implement.** Present the electronic portfolio to the intended target audience.

- **Evaluate.** Evaluate the presentation's effectiveness in light of its purpose and the assessment context.

## Effect on Student Professional Development

Each phase of the e-portfolio development process contributes to student's professional development and lifelong learning. Danielson and Abrutyn (1997) have indicated in this regard:

- **Collection.** Students learn to save artifacts that represent the successes and growth opportunities in their day-to-day learning.

- **Selection.** Students review and evaluate the artifacts they have saved, and identify those that demonstrate achievement of specific standards.

- **Reflection.** Students become reflective practitioners, evaluating their own growth over time and their achievement of the standards, as well as the gaps in their development.

- **Projection.** Students compare their reflections to the standards and performance indicators, and set learning goals for the future. This is the stage that transforms e-portfolio development into professional development and supports lifelong learning.

- **Presentation.** Students share their e-portfolio with their peers. At this stage appropriate public commitments are made to encourage collaboration and commitment to professional development and lifelong learning.

## A MODEL FOR PORTFOLIO DESIGN

The Master's e-Portfolio from the Information and Learning Technologies program at the University of Colorado represents the comprehensive exam for the program and offers a generalized model for portfolio design. Using a rubric (University of Colorado, 2004), three professors must assign a passing grade to the student's e-portfolio in order for the comprehensive exam to be regarded as "pass." An overall judgment of "pass" is given only if there are no revisions to be made. If revisions of e-portfolio items are necessary, the student has one additional opportunity to submit the revised item(s); the revisions must be submitted within one calendar year from the faculty's initial e-portfolio assessment.

**Overview of the Model**

As information and learning technology professionals, students are asked to demonstrate that they have met the six professional responsibilities addressed in the program. This is demonstrated by building the e-portfolio with products or projects developed in the course of the program. Students are expected to include as many items as necessary to demonstrate proficiency in the six responsibilities.

Each e-portfolio item is intended to demonstrate a responsibility and is expected to include the following points of analysis—either in the artifact itself or in an accompanying report:

- **Statement of problem** addressed by the product or project.

- **Analysis of situation**, including the learners or participants, setting, external constraints and opportunities, and a statement of goals or objectives for the product or project.

- **Rationale for approach** or activities, including citations and references when appropriate.

- **Report on results** of the product or project.

- **Evidence pointing to value** or usefulness of the product or project.

- **Reflections on lessons learned** as they relate to the student's professional goals, next steps, and guidelines for use of student's work.

**E-Portfolio Items Representing Responsibilities**

As indicated above, in order to receive a Master's Degree in Information and Learning Technologies from the University of Colorado, it is required that each student complete each of the six responsibilities required of the program. Below is a list of the e-portfolio items which includes the responsibilities demonstrated by each project:

- **Reflection Letter.** The student will write a one to two page reflection letter addressed to the Program Chair, that reflects on what the student has learned in the program—clearly explaining the student's professional goals and how the e-portfolio relates to those goals.

- **Résumé.** The student will develop a résumé detailing the student's experience and credentials for assuming the responsibilities of an information and learning technologist—organized and presented in a professional style.

- **Matrix.** The student will develop a one page matrix that provides an overview of the e-portfolio (Table 1). The top row lists the six responsibilities. The right column lists the projects selected by the student. The Xs identify which responsibility is addressed by each project.

**Table 1**
**Student Matrix Overview of E-Portfolio**

| Responsibility | 1 | 2 | 3 | 4 | 5 | 6 |
|---|---|---|---|---|---|---|
| Project 1 | x | | | x | | x |
| Project 2 | | x | x | x | | |
| Project 3 | | x | | x | x | x |
| Project 4 | x | | | | | |
| Project 5 | | x | x | | x | x |

- **Demonstration of Responsibility #1**. The student will demonstrate continued improvement of professional practice that requires critical inquiry, professional development, and reflective practice (e.g., membership in professional organization, project report on a professional presentation, literature review or critique, collection evaluation).

- **Demonstration of Responsibility #2**. The student will design instruction or human performance strategies to meet the needs of learners (e.g., analysis of problem situation, design of instructional strategy consistent with analysis of situation, use of situated learning models, use of collaborative learning strategies, experience as a knowledge facilitator rather than deliverer).

- **Demonstration of Responsibility #3**. The student will use a variety of media to deliver instruction to students and to engage students in learning (e.g., samples of tools and technologies designed to meet specific needs and objectives).

- **Demonstration of Responsibility #4.** The student will demonstrate s/he understands how to capitalize on the capacities and abilities of each learner (e.g., product or project which accommodates the special social, intellectual, cultural, environmental, and institutional aspects of the learners and their learning situation).

- **Demonstration of Responsibility #5.** The student will manage complex projects and resources in support of learning (e.g., project report on leadership role in a situation which resulted in individual or organizational learning).

- **Demonstration of Responsibility #6:** The student will use incisive and relevant assessment and evaluation techniques (e.g., product or project which uses formative and/or summative evaluations).

- **Production Values.** The student will demonstrate production values for overall presentation, design, and organization. Overall presentation refers to the professional appearance of the e-portfolio. Design refers to the design of text, media presentation, or other formats. Organization refers to how accessible and understandable the portfolio is to the reader/viewer.

The Master's e-Portfolio for the Information and Learning Technologies program at the University of Colorado represents an exemplary alternative assessment method to the existing paradigm of the comprehensive examination. This model is flexible enough to be adapted to fit a variety of traditional or Web-based graduate programs. For example, for the Online Master of Education in Educational Technology at The University of Texas at Brownsville and Texas Southmost College, the educational technology standards from the Association for Educational Communications and Technology can be used in place of the Information and Learning Technologies standards.

## REQUIREMENTS AND CAVEATS
## FOR IMPLEMENTING PORTFOLIOS

Wilkerson and Lang (2003) identified eight requirements and eight caveats for implementing e-portfolios in high-stakes assessment. Table 2 lists requirements for the assessments of e-portfolios and indicates caveats related to their use for institution-based certification or graduation decisions:

**Table 2**
**Requirements for Assessments and Caveats for E-Portfolios**

| Requirements for Assessments | Caveats for E-Portfolios |
|---|---|
| 1. The knowledge and skills to be demonstrated in the e-portfolio must be essential in nature. They must represent important work behaviors that are job-related and be authentic representations of what students do in the real world of work. | Although difficult to substantiate, a justification demonstrating how the preparation of an e-portfolio parallels job-related requirements is necessary. |

| | |
|---|---|
| 2. The e-portfolio assessment must meet the criteria of representativeness, relevance, and proportionality. | All e-portfolio assessment criteria must represent job-related requirements. Criteria such as neatness and organization can be employed if a direct relationship to job performance can be established. |
| 3. There must be adequate procedures and written documents used to provide notice to candidates of the requirements, the appeals process, and the design (fairness) of the appeals process. | An effective process must be implemented to provide information regarding the preparation and evaluation of e-portfolios, including the review process, and due process procedures to challenge review results. |
| 4. There must be adequate instructional opportunities provided to candidates to succeed in meeting the requirements of the e-portfolio and to remediate when performance is inadequate. | e-portfolio preparation should be integrated into the institution's instructional programs. The faculty must support the e-portfolio, and when necessary, provide preparation and consultation opportunities to candidates. |

| | |
|---|---|
| 5. There must be a realistic cut-off score for determining if the performance is acceptable. This cut-off score must differentiate between those who satisfactorily meet the assessment requirements and those who do not. | Determining the criteria and/or characteristics for "pass" and "not pass" for e-portfolios is one of the most challenging procedures in e-portfolio design and implementation. |
| 6. Alternatives must be provided to candidates who cannot successfully complete requirements, or the institution must be able to demonstrate why no alternatives exist. | An equivalent alternative of evidence of performance to an e-portfolio must be identified by the institution. The alternative, however, must maintain the same level of representativeness, relevancy, and proportionality criteria. |
| 7. The results of the e-portfolio evaluation (scoring) and the extent to which protected populations are equally or disproportionately successful must be monitored. | The institution must be prepared to defend its use of the e-portfolio if a disproportionate number of "protected" populations do not successfully complete the e-portfolio process. |

| 8. The process must be implemented and monitored to ensure reliable scoring and to provide for adequate candidate support. | Appropriate documentation must be maintained of *e*-portfolio assessment reliability tests to ensure consistency of scoring procedures, quality and continuity of evaluator training, clarity of directions, and safeguards against cheating. |
|---|---|

## SUMMARY AND CONCLUSIONS

Portfolios have become topics of debate in higher education. While portfolio assessment is prevalent throughout all areas of teacher education, for many educators, the jury is still out on whether or not to use portfolios for high-stakes assessment. The Master's Portfolio from the Information and Learning Technologies program at the University of Colorado represents the comprehensive exam for that program and offers a generalized model for portfolio design.

Portfolio assessments, like all high-stakes tests, must stand the tests of validity, reliability, fairness, and absence of bias. A thorough understanding of the issues surrounding the use of high-stakes assessments requires an appraisal of the potential benefits and risks. The faculty of the online Master of Education in educational Technology at The University of Texas at Brownsville and Texas Southmost College will continue to study the possibility of adopting the e-portfolio as an alternative assessment method to the existing paradigm of the comprehensive examination.

# REFERENCES

Danielson, C., & Abrutyn, L. (1997). *An introduction to using portfolios in the classroom.* Alexandria, VA: Association for Supervision and Curriculum Development.

Ivers, K., & Barron, A.E. (1998). *Multimedia projects in education.* Englewood, CO: Libraries Unlimited.

Salzman, S. A. , Denner, P. R., & Harris, L. R. (2002). *Teacher education outcomes measures: Special study survey.* Washington, D.C.: American Association of Colleges of Teacher Education.

University of Colorado. (2004). *The Master's Portfolio Rubric.* Retrieved August 15, 2004 from http://thunder1.cudenver.edu/ilt/current/library_media/req_portfolio_rubric.htm

Wilkerson, J. R., & Lang, W. S. (2003). Portfolios, the Pied Piper of teacher certification assessments: Legal and psychometric issues. *Education Policy Analysis Archives,* 11(45). Retrieved August 15, 2004 from http://epaa.asu.edu/epaa/v11n45/.

# INTEGRATING BUSINESS ETHICS

# INTO AN UNDERGRADUATE

# BUSINESS CURRICULUM

**David B. Dahlberg**
**Gregory B. Di Novis**
*College of St. Catherine*

## INTRODUCTION

This paper outlines a process and a specific program for integrating ethics across the undergraduate business curriculum that incorporates principles of Catholic social teaching at the College of St. Catherine. It is hoped that such experience can serve as a model for other undergraduate programs in business.

The College of St. Catherine attempts to provides moral guidance dealing with the economic, political and social order. The core themes include the dignity of the human person and human dignity realized in the context of relationships with society and the obligation to love our neighbor, and individual and organizational stewardship of economic and environmental resources.

### Background Information

A literature review identified issues and provided direction for developing a model for integrating ethics into the curriculum. A criticism of undergraduate business programs is that the study of business ethics is treated as a topic which may be taught as a separate course in the philosophy department or the business department; thus not integrating business ethics into business disciplines and decision-making processes. When ethics is integrated in a course, the time spent can be minimal—less than two hours (Rozensher and Fergensen, 1999).

There is support for integrating ethics across the business curriculum (Bishop, 1992; Dunfey and Robertson, 1988; Oddo, 1997; Vallentyne and Accordino, 1998; Rozensher and Fergenson, 1999). However, the literature identifies a number of perceptions or challenges for integrating a program of ethics across the curriculum:

*Challenge 1. Values are already learned before students enter college* (Levin, 1989). However, "students are receptive to information and learning about business ethics" (Crane 2004, p. 151) and favor integrating ethics into a number of courses (Stewart, Felicetti & Kuehn, 1996).

*Challenge 2. Business faculty not trained as philosophers or ethicists may be reluctant to incorporate ethics into their classes* (Oddo, 1997; Loe and Ferrell, 2001). To build faculty confidence in integrating ethics across the curriculum, Virginia Commonwealth University created a faculty development program in which moral theory, professional ethics and teaching practice are covered (Vallentyne and Accordino, 1998).

*Challenge 3. Attitudinal, resource and infrastructure issues need to be identified* (Pharr, 2000). Funding, instructional resources, faculty workloads and incentives all need to be addressed.

*Challenge 4. Subject materials need to be meaningful to students.* Business cases or ethics situations dealing with broad issues at a senior management level are less effective than cases dealing with the conduct of individuals in organizations at entry or early career stage. A variety of experiential, learner-centered approaches should be used in the teaching of ethics such as analysis and discussion of cases, videos and application of business press articles (Loe and Ferrell, 2001).

## INITIAL DEPARTMENTAL SURVEYS

### Student Survey

The authors conducted a short self-administered written survey of their junior and senior year traditional and non-traditional students. Of the 297 students who responded to the survey (approximately 50 percent of all students majoring in business administration) 47 percent were day students and 53 percent were weekend students. Seventeen percent of the respondents to the survey reported that ethical issues were often discussed in their business classes. Seventy-seven percent of the respondents said that ethical issues were discussed in their business courses some of the time. Seventy percent of the survey respondents believed that at this point in their college education they are prepared to make important ethical decisions on the job, but 49 percent of the respondents said that they seldom or never encountered ethical dilemmas in real life.

### Faculty Survey

The business department faculty supported the concept of integrating ethics across the business curriculum. They reported placing significant emphasis on ethics in all introductory courses and on the application of ethics in developing student competency in leadership, working in teams, communications, and application of technology. Faculty indicated that quantifying time spent per course on ethics is "difficult to quantify." All but one faculty member spent less than 20 percent of course time on business ethics and most expressed a desire to increase their emphasis on ethics in all of their courses. They identified the need for teaching/support aids such as case studies, role-playing and videos, and suggested lesson plans for incorporating ethics and a problem-solving framework to help think through ethical issues.

## THE PROGRAM

### Program Goals

The goals of this program were to:

1. Provide a decision model for students to use in recognizing ethical issues and in thinking through ethical issues.

2. Incorporate the basic principles of Catholic social teaching and use the College of St. Catherine values to recognize and resolve ethical issues.

3. Develop a set of discipline specific cases on ethics issues suggested by faculty; cases that are relevant to a variety of organizations that deal with the conduct of individuals in organizations at entry or early career stage.

4. Provide instructors a detailed set of teaching notes for each case.

5. Prepare an instructor's manual that provides suggestions in incorporating ethics into their courses, College of St. Catherine, and teaching with ethics cases.

**Program Issues and Actions**

*Building Faculty Support.* Actions taken included:

- Generated discussion and solicited ideas about how ethics can be incorporated into business courses.

- Identified barriers and attractions and program objectives.

- Developed a proposal and solicited written endorsements from business and theology department faculty.

*Providing Relevant Teaching Material.* Actions taken included:

- Researched and described realistic ethical dilemmas or issues based on actual events that a student might face on the job, usually within in the first five years of their careers.

- Developed discipline specific cases to help students recognize and solve ethical situations and enhance knowledge of the discipline under study.

- Created ambiguity—situations where values conflict. Researched and described realistic ethical dilemmas or issues based on actual events that a student might face on the job, usually within in the first five years of careers.

- Incorporated teaching notes for each case to help the instructor in teaching with the case method.

- Assessed the major learning outcomes.

- Asked faculty members to review and comment on cases specific to their discipline.

- Tested the cases in the classroom (authors incorporated the cases in their class on Organization Ethics in the spring of 2004).

***Reluctance of Business Faculty Not Trained as Philosophers or Ethicists.*** Actions taken included:

- Conducted a faculty workshop to overview the program, provide orientation to College of St. Catherine and to review traditional moral theories and the case teaching method.

- Provided faculty with a resource manual that in addition to the workshop material included bibliography, references to useful Websites and discussion of stakeholder approaches to decision making.

## OUTCOMES AND CONCLUSIONS

General positive findings from the program led the authors to conclude:

- Students' critical thinking skills improved and students were able to incorporate more complexity when dealing with ethical dilemmas and alternative courses of action.

- Students were able to better integrate the knowledge of material from different disciplines instead of examining an ethical situation in isolation.

- Students became more comfortable dealing with ambiguous situations that did not readily lend themselves to a clear right/wrong or win/win solution.

- Students became less frustrated as time went on with the fact that they were required to make decisions in an environment of risk and uncertainty where all the facts were not known.

Some concerns for program improvement included:

- A long-term commitment to the program and significant investment in time and energy in building consensus and in developing business ethics cases appeared necessary. For example, cases did not always work as intended and may require revision. Other experiential teaching approaches need to be pursued such as computer simulations, role-playing and videos.

- Providing students with a brief overview of the basics of College of St. Catherine appeared not to be adequate. The Introduction to Management course seems to be a logical place to introduce organization ethics, College of St. Catherine, and the case method. This issue is currently under a curriculum review process.

## REFERENCES

Bishop, T. (1992). Integrating business ethics into an undergraduate curriculum. *Journal of Business Ethics, 11,* 291-299.

Crane, F. G. (2004). The teaching of business ethics: An imperative at business schools. *Journal of Education for Business, 79*(13), 149-151.

Dunfee, T. W., & Robertson, D. C. (1988). Integrating ethics into the business school curriculum. *Journal of Business Ethics, 7,* 847-859.

Levin, M. (1989, November 20). Ethics courses useless. *The New York Times,* p. A21.

Loe, T. W., & Ferrell, L. (2001). Teaching marketing ethics in the 21$^{st}$ century. *Marketing Education Review, 22*(2), 1-16.

Oddo, A. R. (1997). A framework for teaching business ethics. *Journal of Business Ethics, 16,* 293-297.

Pharr, S. W. (2000). Foundational considerations for establishing an integrated business core curriculum. *Journal of Education for Business, 76*(1), 20-23.

Rozensher, S. G., & Fergenson, P. E. (1999). Faculty perspectives on ethics: A comparison of marketing with other business school faculty. *Marketing Education Review, 9*(1), 51-59.

Stewart, K., Felicetti, L., & Kuehn, S. (1996). The attitudes of business majors toward the teaching of business ethics. *Journal of Business Ethics, 15*, 913-918.

Vallentyne, P., & Accordino, J., (1998). Teaching critical thinking about ethical issues across the curriculum. *Liberal Education, 84* (2), 46-52.

# E-LEARNING OPTIONS

# AND THE CHALLENGES OF CHANGE

**Jeana M. Davis**
*Florida Community College at Jacksonville*

## INTRODUCTION

*What is e-learning?* Many people, when they think of e-learning, think only of Web-based courses. Historically, however, e-learning has encompassed a number of technologies including computer-based training, interactive videodisc and multimedia. The U.S. Military and the Department of Defense made the first attempts to utilize computer-based training, using text to deliver the message to the student. These early attempts used little or no narration, few sound effects and primitive line graphics. The major benefit lay in its ability to harness the power of the computer to process student feedback—something no textbook could do (Jalobeanu, 2003).

Interactive videodisc training came along in the 1970's and was designed to take advantage of the interactive nature of computers using linear motion video. This type of system linked narration with text and video. According to Jalobeanu (2003), many educators debated the merits of reading text in order to learn versus hearing and seeing a presentation. While no clear conclusion was reached, most agreed that training appeared more enjoyable from a mini-movie than from an electronic book. On the downside, this type of training required costly hardware not generally found on most computers of the day.

Multimedia development in the late 1980's and early 1990's was brought about through advancements in video and audio compression, faster central processing units and the development of sophisticated authoring tools and CD-ROM technologies. These new technologies made courseware easier and faster to develop and were ideal for use on the Web (Jalobeanu, 2003).

E-learning, for the purposes of this paper, is loosely defined as the use of Web-based technologies in teaching and learning. This can be divided into several subcategories or learning environments: Web facilitated, blended/hybrid, and fully online courses. Among these there is a great deal of diversity in the course delivery methods that individual instructors can use (Allen & Seaman, 2003) and in the implementation strategies adopted by each institution. According to Rich (2001) the typical characteristics of e-learning include 24/7 accessibility, a learner-centered structure, a focus on problem-solving and analysis rather than memorization, the ability to create links between related topics and themes to enhance integration of theory and practice, and the establishment of synchronous and/or asynchronous communication venues.

**Types of E-Learning Courses**

A survey conducted by the Sloan-C Consortium (Allen & Seaman, 2003) defined e-learning environments as follows (Table 1):

**Table 1**
**E-Learning Environments**

| Proportion of Content Delivered Online | e-Learning Environment | Typical Description |
|---|---|---|
| 1% to 29% | Web facilitated | Course which uses Web-based technology to facilitate what is essentially a face-to-face course. For example, might use Blackboard or WebCT to post the syllabus and assignments. |
| 30% to 79% | Blended/Hybrid | Course that is a blend of the online and face-to-face course. Substantial proportion of the content is delivered online, typically uses online discussions, typically has some face-to-face meetings. |
| 80+% | Fully Online | A course where the vast bulk of the content is delivered online. Typically has no face-to-face meetings. |

**Note.** Adapted from Allen & Seaman (2003).

Courses which use Web-based technology only to facilitate what is essentially a face-to-face course are extremely common; however, these courses make no significant use of the Web for content delivery. Instead, they use technology merely as a delivery tool for the syllabus or assignments. Such courses will not be included in further discussions of e-learning in this paper.

## Institutional Benefits and Barriers to E-Learning

E-learning seems to promise many benefits to the institutions which adopt it, including the potential to reach a larger market of students (Berge & Schrum, 1998), reduced seat time, flexible scheduling, cost savings through use of prepared courses materials (Berg, 2002), and the opportunity to adopt innovative pedagogical approaches (Kanuka, 2002). There are also benefits to students and faculty in the enormous resources which are available at the click of a mouse and in the possibilities for immediate feedback and evaluation through e-mail and online conferencing (Berge & Schrum, 1998).

With such predictions for potential gains it is easy to imagine a rosy future for e-learning in higher education. However, there are barriers to overcome at many institutions. Despite the increasing student demand, many faculty and administrators are still reluctant to accept and use e-learning. According to Allen and Seaman (2003), academic leaders at a majority of institutions (59.6 percent) agree that their faculty accept the value and legitimacy of online education; however, this leaves over 40 percent of institutions that are neutral or disagree with this statement. Berge (1998) identified a list of barriers, including fear of the imminent replacement of faculty by computers, faculty culture, non-educational considerations taking precedence over educational priorities and faculty and administration resistance to change.

*Enrollment Demands.* Today education is a demand-driven commodity. Between 1980 and 2002, college enrollments increased by more than 3.5 million students; almost 45 percent of that increase has been from students 25 years of age or older (Hoffman, 2003). Howell, Williams and Lindsay (2003) estimate that the largest high school class in U.S. history will occur in 2009 and that college enrollments will increase over 16 percent in the next ten years. They postulate that the current higher education infrastructure cannot accommodate the growing college-aged population and enrollments and project that to meet this demand, the annual market for distance learning will grow from it's 2003 level of $4.5 billion to $11 billion by 2005.

The growing student base with a significantly high proportion of non-traditional students generally has multiple demands on time and money—jobs, family, location, class times and costs all have to be weighted in the student's educational decisions and are predicted to lead to an increased demand for non-traditional alternatives which offer greater flexibility for the student (Howell, Williams & Lindsay, 2003). As the demand for non-traditional alternatives in higher education increases, the implications for institutions which have high resistance levels from faculty and administration are serious, and include decreasing enrollments and decreased funding as students gravitate to institutions which will meet their needs.

*What can be done to resolve this situation?* This paper will investigate what e-learning options are available to colleges and universities with regard to learning environments and implementation strategies, why there is still so much resistance to the adoption of e-learning technologies, and possible ways colleges and universities can overcome this resistance and secure administrative and faculty support of e-learning strategies.

# E-LEARNING USAGE IN HIGHER EDUCATION

## E-learning Options

Colleges and universities have a number of options when it comes to e-learning. First there are the e-learning environments mentioned earlier: blended or hybrid courses and fully online courses. These can include instructor-led or instructor-less content delivery in multiple formats including self-paced training, one-to-many virtual events (e.g., virtual classrooms, virtual lecture halls or expert-led discussions), one-to-one mentoring such as help-desks and e-mail exchanges, simulations, both synchronous and asynchronous collaborations (e.g., chat rooms or discussion boards), and course management systems such as Blackboard and WebCT (Jalobeanu, 2003).

Today, most schools offer a combination of environments to meet varying student needs, with nearly 34.5 percent of them offering fully online degree programs, and it appears this trend will continue into the future. When asked about the role of online education for the future of their institution, 67 percent answered that it is a critical long-term strategy (Allen & Seaman, 2003; see Table 2).

**Table 2**
**E-Learning Courses Offered by Institutions of Higher Education, 2002-2003**

|  | Public Institutions | Private, Non-Profit Institutions | Private, For-Profit Institutions | Total Instit utions |
|---|---|---|---|---|
| Both Blended/Hybrid and Online | 80.2% | 36.7% | 21.2% | 55.6% |
| Online Only | 12.5% | 17.8% | 23.7% | 16.0% |
| Blended/Hybrid Only | 3.8% | 17.1% | 6.6% | 9.6% |
| Fully-Online Degree Programs | 48.9% | 22.1% | 20.2% | 34.5% |

**Note.** Adapted from Allen & Seaman (2003)

Such findings are to be expected when one looks at the history of and predictions for e-learning in higher education. In the National Center for Education Statistics report: Distance Education at Postsecondary Education Institutions: 1997-98 (Lewis, et al., 1999) it was reported that 33.53 percent of all 2-year and 4-year Title IV-eligible, degree-granting institutions offered distance education courses during 1997-1998. Nearly 60 percent of those schools used asynchronous Internet-based technologies as a delivery method, up from 22 percent of institutions in 1995.

The follow-up report (Waits & Lewis, 2003) found that in 2000-2001, 56 percent of all 2-year and 4-year Title IV-eligible, degree-granting institutions offered distance education courses and that 90 percent of those institutions used asynchronous Internet-based technologies as the delivery method.

**E-Learning Enrollments**

The Waits & Lewis (2003) report also illustrated the increasing student demand for non-traditional course delivery options with its estimate of 3.1 million enrollments in distance education courses in 2000-2001, up from the 1.6 million enrollments reported for 1997-98. Allen and Seaman (2003) also predict continued growth in e-learning enrollments, projecting an overall growth rate of nearly 20 percent in the number of students studying online from Fall 2002 to Fall 2003 (Table 3).

**Table 3**
**Students Taking at Least One Online Course:**
**Fall 2002 and Projected Fall 2003**

| Total Students Fall 2002 | Projected Students Fall 2003 | Percentage Growth |
|---|---|---|
| 1,602,970 | 1,920,734 | 19.8% |

**Note.** Adapted from Allen & Seaman (2003)

## COURSE/PROGRAM DEVELOPMENT OPTIONS

Colleges and universities also have several options with regard to acquiring or developing e-learning courses and programs including the purchase of off-the-shelf courses from publishers and courseware developers, in-house course development where schools choose to develop the courses and materials themselves, or collaborative efforts with other institutions. The choices an institution makes in this regard are dependent upon a number of factors. The following is a partial list of considerations identified by Dwyer (1999) as part of his needs assessment plan:

- Is the technical expertise available to develop and sustain the system

- Are the principals involved inclined towards teamwork

- Are the processes of project management understood (gant charts, resource allocation, etc.)

- Is there a budget available for internal/external consulting and materials development

- Will the subject matter specialist be able to contribute a sufficient amount of time to the project

- Will the subject matter specialist be available to sustain, make revisions and update the content material

- Is adequate training available for all principals involved

- Will the courses be delivered synchronously, asynchronously or both

- Has the course been taught before or will it have to be developed from scratch

- What are the goals or objectives to be achieved by the course

Based on their needs, some schools elect to utilize all three methods or some combination thereof. Florida

Community College at Jacksonville, for example, develops many of it's own for-credit online courses, sometimes including even writing their own textbooks for those courses. They also work in collaboration with various consortial groups to jointly develop courses for both undergraduate and graduate level programs. Like many institutions they also purchase licenses to offer "canned" courses in their curriculums. The majority of these latter offerings are continuing education courses rather than "credit" academic offerings.

**In House Course Development**

There are special considerations for institutions which choose to develop their own courses either on their own or as part of a consortium. According to Brown (2003), in-house development is important because it helps to overcome the 'not invented here' syndrome. It also has many benefits for the institution: in-house course development provides an opportunity for the institution to showcase strengths in particular disciplines, it can be less expensive than purchasing the materials elsewhere and it opens up opportunities for revenue generation. Disadvantages of the in-house approach include the amount of time and resources required to develop a critical mass of material.

Brown (2003) identifies a number of key factors for success including:

- Initial funding to support faculty release time for the project

- Maintaining centralized control over project budgets

- Situating project ownership with the developing faculty to maintain commitment and enthusiasm during the development phase and providing a receptive environment for adoption upon completion

- Establishing the Internet as the primary delivery method and learner support medium in order to set priorities for infrastructure investment, software tools and staff development

- Concentrating on readily available, familiar development tools which can be supported in-house

- Providing highly skilled technical support resources for course design and production

*The UK's E-Campus Experience.*   At the UK's e-Campus, it was hoped that removing some of the constraints on time and place of study would make it easier for part-time and non-traditional students to study. This was expected to open up opportunities for disadvantaged groups and to reduce drop-out rates for all types of students (Brown, 2002).

The UK's E-Campus decided to produce most of its courses and materials internally. It was conceived as a top-down, management-led initiative. Faculty were assigned to work closely with educational technologists to develop specific proposed courses. Key steps in the development process included the development of appropriate teaching, learning and assessment strategies; the identification and acquisition of resource-based learning materials; the development of teaching and learning materials and activities; the identification of staff development needs and implementation of staff development solutions; and the application of appropriate resources such as graphic design, courseware authoring, programming, desktop publishing, audio, video, photography, digitization, printing, etc. (Brown, 2003)

The implementation of their program was dependent upon five key policy decisions: 1) a single delivery medium (the Internet was chosen for its cross platform independence); 2) specific software standards for authoring, assessment and conferencing; 3) centralized project funding and monitoring; 4) local project management; and 5) centralized media production resources. Faculty involved in the project were offered a combination of formal training events, including Web-authoring skills, course platform training and informal on the job support in the areas of learning objectives, assessment strategies, teaching methods and learner characteristics (Brown, 2003).

Brown concluded that the E-Campus project was generally successful, but did suffer from problems related to changes in the organizational environment and the lack of understanding with regard to the costs of developing a virtual online presence. In the first 22 months of the project, over 30 different courses were established. Students started to study the first of these during the first semester of 1998 and by 2000 more than 3,000 students were enrolled in these courses. Feedback from the students overall was positive (Brown, 2003).

## The Challenges Of Change

According to Brown (2003), migration from face-to-face teaching methods to hybrid and online course delivery is more than just a technical challenge. It also requires cultural change. Brown also identifies four areas of activity critical to E-Campus' successful transformation from a traditional face-to-face environment to an e-learning environment:

- Faculty strategic development planning

- Quality assurance

- Staff rewards

- Staff development

## CONSORTIAL EFFORTS

A major challenge associated with online course and program development is the lack of resources—financial, technical and human (Fleming, Tammone & Wahl, 2002). Many institutions choose to meet that challenge by engaging in consortial efforts to develop their programs and courses. This paper will examine two such efforts, the Michigan Community College Virtual Learning Collaborative and the Colorado Electronic Community College.

### The Michigan Community College Virtual Learning Collaborative

This effort identified three major challenge areas in order to offer an e-learning program—development, delivery and student support. They found that Michigan community colleges each offered a limited selection of online courses, but none had all the courses available to complete an online program of study at a single college. They also acknowledged that faculty who taught these online courses had multiple demands on their time including teaching their online courses, developing new online courses and, quite often, teaching traditional face-to-face courses. These responsibilities resulted in limitations in the number of online sections a particular college could offer. The Michigan community colleges also found that providing academic and student support services such as library resources, academic counseling, financial aid, tutoring and course assessment services was a constant challenge (Fleming et al., 2002).

To address these challenges, the Michigan community colleges turned to collaboration and emerging information technologies which made it possible for them to work together in new ways. The voluntary program began in 1997 and the first two years were spent in identifying strategic goals for the collaborative and preparing a business plan which involved the development and adoption of a home college/provider college model with course delivery by the provider college and some support services provided by the home college. It also established a general framework for cooperation in course development and delivery, as well as professional development opportunities and student support services (Fleming et al., 2002).

The business plan (Fleming et al., 2002) provided a blueprint for the future of the collaborative which included

- Home college responsibilities

- Provider college responsibilities

- Tuition structure for online courses

- Tuition sharing between the provider and home colleges

- Articulation agreement

- Financial aid agreement

- Guidelines for the online programs of study

The results of these efforts has been an offering of 453 courses in Fall 2001 by 25 of the 28 Michigan community colleges, with 15 complete online certificate or degree programs and enrollment of more than 8,300 students in those courses. The courses are all accessed through a single Web site along with full academic and student support services (Fleming et al, 2002)—see Table 4.

**Table 4**
**Michigan Community College Virtual Learning Collaborative Enrollment Trends**

|  | Provider Colleges | Courses Available | Total Enrollments |
|---|---|---|---|
| Summer 1999 | 12 | 47 | >700 |
| Fall 1999 | 17 | 133 | >1800 |
| Winter 2000 | 19 | 203 | >3200 |
| Summer 2000 | 14 | 100 | >1660 |
| Fall 2000 | 22 | 285 | >4450 |
| Winter 2001 | 22 | 296 | >5200 |
| Summer 2001 | 17 | 174 | >3280 |
| Fall 2001 | 22 | 453 | >8300 |
| Winter 2002 | 25 | >500 | Not Reported |

**Note.** Adapted from Fleming., Tammone, & Wahl (2002).

A further benefit to the Michigan community colleges has been the ability to offer frequent, high quality professional development activities for all colleges in the consortium at per-college costs which are substantially less than those colleges would face if they provided similar training on their own. More than 800 faculty, staff and administrators participated in that training during 2000 and 2001 (Fleming at al, 2002).

While the consortium members feel they have found a successful model for meeting the challenges of online program development, program and course delivery and student support services, examination of the process by the consortial committee has identified several areas to be addressed in the future. These include the development of a more streamlined transcript process (there is no common course numbering system in Michigan), implementation of an assessment standard and development of a process for updating collaboratively developed courses and programs (Fleming et al, 2002).

### The Colorado Electronic Community College

.   The Colorado Community College and Occupational Health Educational System provides higher education opportunities to over 90,000 credit students each year from a population of over four million statewide. The system identified a major challenge in serving students equitably in remote rural or mountainous regions and also recognized that courses offered by individual members of the system which did not meet minimum enrollments were cancelled, regardless of the need for the courses. They determined that a partnership of colleges which offered shared courses across the colleges in an easily accessible electronic format would minimize and possibly eliminate these problems. The 12-member Colorado Community College Online was developed to meet those needs (Seehusen, 2000).

The original consortium committee was made up of the presidents of the 12 member institutions. The committee reached an agreement to create an online degree Web site and utilized a local vendor who had experience creating online college sites. They also selected The Colorado Electronic Community College to manage the creation of the site, in part because it was not a competitor of any one of the system colleges. Once the program was up and running the presidents realized that decision-making authority should rest with those who are in the position of dealing with it on a daily basis, so the vice presidents of instruction and student services were given policy-making and policy-changing authority. Unlike the Michigan consortium committee which meets 12 times a semester via interactive videoconferencing, the Colorado committee maintain weekly communications through newsletters and meet face-to-face every six to eight weeks (Seehusen, 2000).

The program requires students to enroll in these online classes through The Colorado Electronic Community College Web site. The data are uploaded nightly to the main system computer then separated by college and uploaded to the individual college computers. Every online course offered through the online site is listed in the schedule of every member college (Seehusen, 2000).

A key difference in the Colorado case when compared to Michigan is the structure of the consortium. In Michigan, they use a provider college/home college approach. The Colorado consortium elected to establish a governing body in The Colorado Electronic Community College which would manage all of the online courses with each of the member institutions relating directly to the consortium rather than to each other. The Colorado Electronic Community College determined that tuition income for the online courses would be split between the home college, the Web site vendor, faculty pay and a management fee to the consortium (Seehusen, 2000).

Seehusen (2000) does not provide enrollment figures for the program, but does report that enrollments are increasing in the online program with each semester and that needed classes no longer have to be cancelled due to low enrollments. Seehusen also reports that a number of critical lessons have been learned during the implementation of the program.

One key finding is that the delivery of seamless instructional and student services online is simplified by creating teams that cut across departmental lines. These teams must have a clear understanding of their responsibilities. They have also learned that traditional student services often do not translate well into an online environment. Student services staff must be trained to provide clear, concise and correct information to the students with little margin for error. They must also be prepared to be cross-functional so that students are not shuffled from one e-mail address to another.

While structurally different, it is clear that the two different approaches to managing consortial efforts had similar goals, results and challenges. Each found that the individual member institutions realized significant savings in course development costs, training costs and program development costs. Each also realized significant benefits for the institutions and for their students in terms of more viable course offerings, increased enrollments, and greater accessibility.

## THE ADMINISTRATION, THE FACULTY
## AND OVERCOMING RESISTANCE

While it might be easy to think that colleges and universities exist solely to provide higher education opportunities to the population and the administration and faculty work together as a team to meet that need, in reality, it's a completely different story. Many universities have a research mission which overrides the education mandate (Florida, 1999). Community colleges are generally expected to fulfill the workforce education needs of a given community and prepare the academically inclined student for the university environment (Kasper, 2002-03).

Administrators and faculty, likewise, have divergent roles. Administrators traditionally are concerned with governance, advancement of the institution and with the institution's relationship to the community. Faculty are traditionally more concerned with teaching and research. Naturally, these different areas have different concerns when it comes to the selection, implementation and management of e-learning programs.

## Administration Concerns

"When resources are scarce and time a precious commodity, peers become competitors and tradition becomes sacred ground" (Ellis, 2000, p. 238). The world of academia has always been steeped in tradition and many college and university administrators have come to see technology as a distinct threat to their traditions and all that they stand for. Full integration of e-learning programs in the institution's strategic plan requires significant cultural change (Berge & Muilenberg, 2001), something which does not come about easily.

Levy (2001) claims that higher education administrators are very much interested in Internet-based distance education programs in hopes they will become more competitive and more cost efficient, but many administrators seem to have particularly strong feelings against the integration of e-learning programs into the research university environment. Ellis (2000) quotes one Penn State administrator as saying "I personally don't really think that on-load teaching of World Campus courses will work at a research university where the priorities are strongly driven toward research, external funding, and various other kind of things" (Ellis, 2000, p. 238). As research is a driving force behind much of a university's funding (Florida, 1999), this area of resistance can be a difficult one to overcome.

Berge (1998) divides the perceived administrative barriers to e-learning reported in his survey into nine broad and by no means exhaustive areas: academic, fiscal, geographic service area, governance, labor/management, legal, student support services, technical and cultural. In identifying concerns in each of these areas Berge feels that online learning could fail unless academic administrators provide the support needed to fully handle these challenges and overcome barriers as needed.

A quick glance down the list (Table 5) reveals that many of the concerns of the administrator which need to be considered with regard to e-learning applications need also to be considered for face-to-face learning. However, there are a number of areas which are seriously complicated with the advent of e-learning and the resultant expansion into new student markets. Further, many of the needed changes such as state regulations, regional limitations and existing structure vs. shadow colleges or enclaves are beyond the scope of the college or university administrator to change and require policy change at the governmental level.

**Table 5**
**Key Barriers to Online Teaching**

| Policy Development Area | Key Issues |
|---|---|
| Academic | Academic calendar<br>Course integrity<br>Course transferability<br>Evaluation process<br>Admission standards<br>Curriculum approval process<br>Accreditation |

| Fiscal | Tuition rate |
|--------|--------------|
| | Technology fee |
| | FTE's (full time enrollments) |
| | Consortia contracts |
| | State regulations |
| Geographic Service Area | Regional limitations |
| | Local vs. out-of-state tuition |
| | Consortia agreements |
| Governance | Single vs. multiple board oversight |
| | Staffing |
| | Existing structure vs. shadow colleges or enclaves |
| Labor Management | Compensation and workload |
| | Development incentives |
| | Intellectual property |
| | Faculty development and training |
| | Congruence with existing union contracts |
| Legal | Fair use and copyright |
| | Faculty, student and institutional liability |
| Student Support | Advisement and counseling |
| | Library access |
| | Test proctoring |
| Technical | Lack of systems reliability/connectivity/access |
| | Inadequate hardware/software |
| | Inadequate infrastructure |
| | Inadequate technical support |
| Cultural | Faculty or student resistance to innovation |
| | Resistance to online teaching methods |
| | Difficulty recruiting faculty |
| | Lack of understanding about distance education and what works at a distance |

**Note.** Adapted from Berge (1998).

**Faculty Concerns**

Traditionally, the faculty role contains three functions: research, teaching and service (Paulson, 2002). However, under most conditions an individual faculty member can carry out five distinct activities when delivering instruction:

- Designing the course or curriculum

- Developing the course or curriculum by selecting appropriate instructional methods and course materials, or creating those course materials

- Delivering the subject matter through lectures or the use of various forms of media

- Mediating the learning process (tutoring)

- Assessing individual student learning through assignments, projects, quizzes, papers and exams (Paulson, 2002).

According to O'Quinn and Corry (2002), many facets of faculty's roles have changed as a result of advances in educational technology. Faculty have had to adapt to new ways of teaching and communicating with their students requiring a paradigm shift in how they orchestrate and facilitate the act of learning. One of the problems many faculty face in this regard is that their training was concentrated in content areas rather than in curriculum design and lesson planning.

*How do faculty themselves view these problems and what barriers do they see to overcoming them?* A number of recent studies and surveys have been conducted in this area (Berge, 1998; Berge & Muilenberg, 2001; Cookson,

2000; Ellis, 2000; Folkestad & Haag, 2002; Howell, Williams & Lindsay, 2003; O'Quinn and Corry, 2002; Parker, 2003). Not surprisingly, they all report similar findings. The barriers and concerns which appear throughout all of these surveys include:

- Time

- Compensation

- Issues of tenure and advancement

- Assessment

- Intellectual property rights

- Administrative structure and support

- Intangible rewards such as personal satisfaction and a sense of community

- Fear of technology.

*Time.* Time, specifically the lack of time to develop courses and the significant increase in time needed to teach online courses as opposed to traditional classroom courses was cited in every study as a major barrier to faculty participation in e-learning programs. Faculty find that they have to update and refine their e-learning courses every year or two to remain competitive; this also requires investigating new technologies (Folkestad & Haag, 2002). The Berge study (1998) cites the lack of an adequate time frame to implement online courses and increased time required for both online contacts and preparation of materials and activities. According to Cookson (2000) Web-based online education is very time consuming. If faculty don't get incentives, they will not teach on the Web. O'Quinn and Corry (2002) also cited lack of time and the heavy workload as the major reason faculty would not participate in distance education.

The Berge and Muilenberg study (2001) examined colleges and universities at five distinct stages of e-learning organization and determined that faculty compensation and the lack of development and maintenance time are the greatest barriers to distance education across all organizational stages. Ellis (2000) reported that release time for faculty to develop new courses was the top incentive for faculty participation in e-learning programs at Pennsylvania State University World Campus. A study by Howell, Williams and Lindsay (2003) echoed the findings of the Ellis report quoting an NEA survey that reported that faculty members' top concern about distance education was that they would be required to do more work for the same amount of pay. The study found that most faculty members do spend more time on their distance courses than on traditional courses and that 84 percent do not get a reduced workload.

To further press down on the time issue, in a review of 102 articles on motivations and incentives for distance learning faculty (Parker, 2003), it was reported that 95 of those articles cited decreased workload and 86 cited release time to develop and teach online courses as significant motivators and incentives. In the case of workload, the article defined it in two ways—first as the number of courses taught each semester and alternately from the perspective of class size, which affects the amount of time needed for each class.

*Compensation.* Directly related to the time issue, of course, is the issue of compensation. Parker (2003) reports that of the 102 articles surveyed in the above study, 98 of them listed compensation as the major incentive to participation in e-learning programs. Parker also noted that while stipends are the most requested reward, they are not supported by over half of the nation's colleges.

Folkestad & Haag (2002) found that faculty fail to participate in e-learning because they are not rewarded financially. The study also found that when this idea was discussed with administrators, some administrators did not understand the pedagogical difference between teaching a class face-to-face and teaching it online, so they were unable to comprehend the need for additional financial remuneration for teaching online courses.

*Tenure.* Another major barrier, especially for new faculty and those at research institutions, is the impact (or lack thereof) that online teaching can have on the tenure process. Ellis (2000) quoted one Penn State administrator as saying "I would not recommend any non-tenured faculty member do that [teach in the World Campus]. I might say to that faculty member, you should be out writing grant proposals or you should be writing your new book because this is going to get you the reputation from Penn State. It's going to elevate the college" (Ellis, 2000, p. 236).

*Assessment and Intellectual Property Rights.* Many faculty also expressed concerns with regard to assessment and academic integrity. Faculty worried that students might be cheating by having other students do their online work (Howell et al., 2003; Levy, 2001). Intellectual property rights, specifically the ownership of courses developed by faculty who do not receive any additional recompense for that work, was also an issue for many faculty (Berge & Muilenberg, 2001; Folkestad & Haag, 2002; Howell et al., 2003).

## OVERCOMING RESISTANCE

As the demand for e-learning continues to increase, some schools and governments are taking an aggressive approach to dealing with these concerns. Some examples follow.

## St. Petersburg College

St. Petersburg College has developed a benchmarking program to allow it to address each of the areas of concern and others which they have identified through an evaluation process of their e-learning practices (Burkhart, 2001). By first identifying problems on a national and worldwide level and then evaluating the College's response to that problem, St. Petersburg College has been able to develop a proactive plan for identifying and overcoming obstacles to e-learning at their institution.

## Fort Scott Community College

Fort Scott Community College developed a plan to systematically implement technology throughout the college and have all academic areas offering online courses as a part of their accreditation process (Cummings & Buzzard, 2002). The College funded its plan through the aggressive pursuit of grants from federal, state and private sources. They also formed partnerships with other colleges and with industry to gain needed personnel and equipment. Fort Scott Community College provides ongoing small-group, hands-on training to teach new skills and to sharpen skills and troubleshoot problems users might have. They also use grant funds to create "camps" for faculty to assist them in incorporating technological resources and exploring different learning styles and various teaching methods.

**Athabasca University**

In Canada, the provincial government of Alberta established Athabasca University as a non-traditional university in an effort to overcome centuries of tradition in higher education (Cookson, 2000). Athabasca University's mandate requires it to contribute to the post-secondary system by implementing distance education techniques as its core business. The institution's policies answer the concerns still faced by traditional colleges and universities such as promotion and tenure, intellectual property, infrastructure, technical support, faculty development, assessment, student support services, research on online teaching, and competition.

**"Expert" Views**

Oblinger (2001) suggests that managing the value chain of higher education might answer a number of problems. She identifies the higher education value chain as the interrelationship between curriculum development, content development, learner acquisition and support, learning delivery, assessment and advising, articulation and credentialing. She argues that while historically institutions of higher education have provided the entire value chain for students, today there are a number of new entrants in the market which can provide some of these services and that in order to effectively manage the value chain and remain competitive, higher education institutions must learn to collaborate with these new entities.

*What does this mean to administrators and faculty?* By partnering with educational publishers, colleges can remove some of the burden for content development from their faculty and allowing them more time to actually teach their courses. By partnering with a full-service broker, administrators can outsource some of their market research and recruiting activities. Partnerships with testing organizations such as ETS can be used to outsource assessment activities.

Paulson (2002) suggests that acquiring and nurturing a new kind of para-professional staff to support instructional development might be the answer to a number of concerns. According to Paulson, these para-professionals need to be technologically skilled, schooled in various pedagogical approaches, and sufficiently knowledgeable in the disciplines to be credible with faculty. The use of these para-professionals can help alleviate workload problems and can also prove beneficial in the planning of future forms of instructional delivery, leading to better outcomes and lower costs.

The most prominent ideas expressed in the literature for overcoming resistance, though, are those which directly answer the most prominent concerns: providing release time for faculty to develop new courses (Ellis, 2000; Howell, Williams & Lindsay, 2003; O'Quinn & Corry, 2002; Parker, 2003), hiring additional new faculty or teaching assistants (Ellis, 2000), paying stipends to faculty who develop new courses (Folkestad & Haag, 2002; O'Quinn & Corry, 2002; Parker, 2003), and enacting policy changes which take online teaching and course development into account for tenure and promotion and which grant intellectual property rights to course developing faculty (Ellis, 2000; Folkestad & Haag, 2002; O'Quinn & Corry, 2002).

## CONCLUSIONS

It is clear from a study of the statistics on record and the projections for the future that the demand for more flexible educational alternatives such as e-learning will continue to increase. Institutions which fail to meet this demand will be faced with declining enrollments and decreased funding in the face of increasing competition. In order to compete, colleges and universities must embrace e-learning as a part of their strategic plan.

This paper has examined the options available to higher education institutions with regard to the selection, implementation and management of e-learning programs. Of the three options identified, the purchase of off-the-shelf courseware is the least viable for most institutions due in large part to the limited selection available. The other two options, in-house development and consortial collaborations, each have significant benefits and drawbacks.

An institution with significant in-house technical expertise and high student demand for courses might do well on their own, developing courses for themselves completely in-house. On the other hand, in today's tight economy an institution with limited in-house technical expertise and significant class cancellations due to insufficient enrollments would probably do better working in a consortial environment where resources and the marketplace could be shared. The two consortial cases discussed in this paper, while structurally different, each realized significant cost savings, increased enrollments and also provided greater access for their students.

This paper has also identified and discussed the challenges faced by administration and faculty with regard to e-learning and how these challenges might be met. Most notable among the perceived administrative challenges are decisions regarding tuition rate and sharing, accreditation, course integrity and transferability, FTE's, governance, staff and faculty compensation, intellectual property issues, consortial agreements and student support.

From the faculty viewpoint, resistance to e-learning will continue until changes are made in the way workload and compensation are calculated, issues of tenure, promotion and intellectual property are dealt with, and intangible rewards such as personal satisfaction and a sense of community are felt. It's clear that the change from a traditional face-to-face, "chalk and talk" teaching environment to an e-learning environment is, for most institutions, a gamma level change requiring cultural change as well as changes in pedagogy, policies, technology, tasks and people.

How institutions approach meeting these needs will vary depending in large part upon how much the administration is willing to invest and how much outside assistance (both governmental and in partnership with business) they can get or will want. The aggressive stances taken by St. Petersburg College and Athabasca University suggest that an institution which focuses on e-learning as an important part of it's long-term strategy can find the funding, develop the policies and enact a viable management plan which meets the needs of the institution, the administration, the faculty and the students, even though in many cases it requires significant structural change.

**Managerial Implications**

While there will always be a need for the face-to-face classroom, there is also a growing need for e-learning alternatives to that classroom. *What does this mean for educational leaders?*

For institutions that do not have an e-learning program in place it means performing a needs assessment to determine whether or not the school should institute an e-learning program. They must first define their mission and their target market, accurately assess their capabilities to deliver the desired educational products to that market to meet that mission, and determine what educational needs they are not meeting for that market within their mission.

Then they can make a determination regarding the value to the institution of going after those unmet needs.

If there is sufficient value to warrant the development, implementation and management of an e-learning program, a second needs assessment needs to be performed to determine which approach—in-house development or a consortial effort—is appropriate based on the resources available to the institution. Each area of concern must be examined including funding, staffing, infrastructure and equipment, training, program management, program marketing, course development, compensation, implementation, student support services, intellectual property rights and quality assessment.

Finally, in order to perpetuate and advance their e-learning programs, educational leaders should be ever vigilant with regard to seeking out and countering pockets of resistance from administrators and faculty. Depending on the needs and resources of the institution this can include policy changes, creative staffing, financial incentives, workload adjustments or any other feasible response. The key here is to find ways to meet the intrinsic and extrinsic needs of the workforce (administrators, faculty and staff) while fulfilling the mission of providing for the educational needs of the student body.

## REFERENCES

Allen, I. E., & Seaman, J. (2003). *Sizing the opportunity: The quality and extent of online education in the United States, 2002 and 2003.* (Sloan Center for Online Education Report). Needham, MA: Sloan-C.

Berg, G. A. (2002). *Why distance learning? Higher education administrative practices.* Westport, CT: Praeger.

Berge, Z. L. (1998). Barriers to online teaching in post-secondary institutions: Can policy changes fix it? *Online Journal of Distance Learning Administration, 1*(2).

Berge, Z. L. & Muilenburg, L. (2001). Obstacles faced at various stages of capability regarding distance education in institutions of higher education. *TechTrends, 45*(4), 40-45.

Berge, Z. L., & Schrum, L. (1998). Linking strategic planning with program implementation for distance education. *Cause/Effect, 21*(3), 31-38.

Brown, S. (2002). Re-engineering the university. *Open Learning, 17*(3), 231-243.

Burkhart, J. (2001.) *How do SPJC administrative and support systems and procedures need to change in order to overcome organizational obstacles to e-learning access? A Report to Leadership, St. Petersburg, FL.* (ERIC Document Reproduction Service No. ED469360)

Cookson, P. (2000). Implications of Internet technology for higher education: North American perspectives. *Open Learning, 15*(1), 71-80.

Cummings, D., & Buzzard, C. (2002). Technology, students and faculty... how to make it happen! Techniques. *Association for Career and Technical Education, 77*(8), 31-33.

Dwyer, F. (1999). Distance education: An evolving instructional technology application. *Educational Media International, 36*(4), 248-257.

Ellis, E. (2000). Faculty participation in the Pennsylvania State University world campus: Identifying barriers to success. *Open Learning, 15*(3), 233-242.

Fleming, T., Tammone, W., & Wahl, M. (2002). *E-learning: Addressing the challenges via collaboration.* (ERIC Document Reproduction Service No. ED 467854).

Florida, R. (1999). The role of the university: Leveraging talent, not technology. In L. M. Branscomb, F. Kodama, & R. Florida (Eds.), *Industrializing knowledge: University linkages in Japan and United States* (pp. 363-373). Cambridge, MA: MIT Press.

Folkestad, L. S., & Haag, S. (2002). *Conflicting ideologies and the shift to e-learning.* Paper presented at the annual meeting of the American Educational Research Association, New Orleans, LA. (ERIC Document Reproduction Service No. ED 464102).

Hoffman, C.M. (2003*). Mini-digest of education statistics: 2002, NCES 2003-061.* Washington, D.C.: U.S. Department of Education, National Center for Education Statistics.

Howell, S. L., Williams, P. B. & Lindsay, N. K. (2003). Thirty-two trends affecting distance education: An informed foundation for strategic planning. *Online Journal of Distance Learning Administration, 6*(3).

Jalobeanu, M. (2003). The Internet in education: The past, the present and, hopefully, the future. In N. Nistor, S. English, S. Wheeler, & M. Jalobeanu (Eds.), *Toward the virtual university: International online perspectives* (pp. 23-36). Greenwich, CT: Information Age Publishing.

Kanuka, H. (2002). Guiding principles for facilitating higher levels of Web-based distance teaching and learning in post-secondary settings. *Distance Education, 23*(2), 163-182.

Kasper H. T. (2002-03). The changing role of community college. *Occupational Outlook Quarterly, 46*(4), 14-21.

Lewis, L., Snow, K., Farris, E., & Levin, D. (1999) *Distance education at degree-granting postsecondary institutions: 1997-98, NCES 2000-013.* Washington, D.C.: U.S. Department of Education, National Center for Education Statistics

Levy, Y. (2001). *E-learning: An overview of next-generation internet based distance learning systems.* In WebNet 2001: World Conference on the WWW and Internet Proceedings, Orlando, FL. (ERIC Document Reproduction Service No. ED 466604).

Oblinger, D. (2001). Will e-business shape the future of open and distance learning? *Open Learning, 16*(1), 9-25.

O'Quinn, L. & Corry, M. (2002). Factors that deter faculty from participating in distance education. *Online Journal of Distance Learning Administration, 5*(4).

Parker, A. (2003). Motivation and incentives for distance faculty. *Online Journal of Distance Learning Administration, 6*(3).

Paulson, K. (2002). Reconfiguring faculty roles for virtual settings. *The Journal of Higher Education, 73*(1), 123-140.

Rich, T. (2001). E-learning futures: Report of an AUA study group. *Perspectives: Policy & Practice in Higher Education, 5*(3) 68-77.

Seehusen, V. (2000). A consortial approach to distance education delivery and management. *Community College Journal of Research & Practice, 24*(1), 27-36.

Waits, T., & Lewis, L. (2003) *Distance education at degree-granting postsecondary institutions: 2000-2001, NCES 2003-017.* Washington, D.C.: U.S. Department of Education, National Center for Education Statistics

# TEACHING FOR LEARNING

# IN THE COMMUNITY COLLEGE:

# INTEGRATING THE SCHOLARSHIP OF

# TEACHING AND LEARNING,

# INFORMATION LITERACY AND TECHNOLOGY

**Ruby Evans**
*University of Central Florida*

## INTRODUCTION

In large part, due to his seminal text, *Scholarship Reconsidered: Priorities of the Professoriate*, Ernest Boyer (1990) directed attention to the scholarship of teaching and learning. McKinney (2004) suggested, however, that informal work pertaining to the scholarship of teaching and learning and its related concepts had occurred for more than three decades. In their text, Lyons, McIntosh and Kysilka (2002) asserted that college teaching in an age of accountability has initiated a renewed call for educational reform. Unlike prior reform initiatives, the focus of those today is not teaching, nor learning, nor even teaching and learning. Rather, the current priority, particularly at the community college, emphasizes teaching for learning.

More recently, with the paradigm shift from teaching-centered to learning-centered institutions (O'Banion, 1997), teaching and learning scholars have begun to reiterate the fallacy of divorcing research and scholarship from teaching (Boyer, 1990; Glassick, Huber & Maeroff, 1997). Boyer proclaimed the relative importance of having campuses where the scholarship of teaching is a

81

central mission and he suggested that faculty, especially those in the community college, should be authorities on how students learn. "Understanding students is a necessary condition for successful teaching" (Murray, 2002, p. 90).

Sperling (2003) stated that "the goal of the scholarship of teaching and learning (SoTL) is ultimately to enhance student learning" (p. 600), adding that the scholarship of teaching and learning connects the dots among students, teachers, teaching strategies, and learning theory and recognizes these faculty as the life-long learners they need to be. Huba and Freed posited that faculty "do not have all of the answers and may need to learn along with their students" (as cited in Warren, 2003, p. 722), with King (2001) suggesting that classroom practice and reflection prompt professors to think about new ways of teaching and learning. Brookfield (2002) admonishes faculty to view teaching practice through four complementary lenses—students' eyes, colleagues' perceptions, educational literature and their autobiographical experiences as learners—to develop a critically reflective stance toward the practice of community college teaching. Levinson (2003) agreed, challenging these faculty members to take a constructivist view of their daily work, thereby becoming reflective practitioners whose efforts have a demonstrable practical bent in classroom settings.

## INFORMATION LITERACY

The League for Innovation in the Community College has identified information management and technology skills as core competencies for student learning outcomes in the twenty-first century (Wilson, Miles, Baker & Schoenberger, 2000). Information literacy may be operationally defined as the ability to access, evaluate, and use information from varied sources (Kasowitz-Scheer, &

Pasqualoni, 2002; Sophos, 2003). Additionally, a number of accrediting and professional associations, including the Southern Association of Colleges and Schools (SACS), have recently identified information literacy as a key outcome for students.

In its publication, "Criteria for Accreditation," SACS stated "[Efforts] should be consistent with the goal of helping students develop information literacy—the ability to locate, evaluate, and use information to become independent life-long learners" (SACS, 1996, Sections 5.1.2.4).

Ereegovac and Yamasaki (1998) declared that community colleges, in their unique role as gateways to higher education, have a singularly important role in equipping students with the core skills and competencies necessary for success in an Information Age. "Educators need to prepare students for a technical world requiring self-initiative in learning, precision in processes, and the ability to identify and analyze pertinent information" (AL-Bataineh & Brooks, 2003, p. 482). Based on their research findings, Profeta and Kendrick (2002) argue that students need to be information literate to navigate the explosion and wealth of information available online.

## INFORMATION TECHNOLOGY

Information technology has changed the way people live and learn, and it continues to significantly impact the infrastructure of formal education and its delivery. The discourse surrounding technology usage in the community college has focused on "how to provide better service to students, while enhancing the culture of learning for students via increased instructor access, better knowledge management, and distributed learning opportunities" (Miller & Pope, 2003, p. 16). Professional development that enables faculty to incorporate information technology into teaching and learning to support instruction is one of the most important challenges in the United States (Cooley & Johnstone, 2001). Floyd (2003) argues that by skillful investment in professional development programs, community colleges leaders can facilitate the successful transformation of campuses into centers of technology-based learning.

Floyd noted that distance education is in line with the institutional mission of access and equity and, hence, must be incorporated. Similarly, Pemberton (2001) argued that distance learning is cost and time effective, accessible and flexible, and that varying student populations and a changing economy make distance education a vital new tool.

With the infusion of technology, faculty are expected to become competent in the use of available learning technologies and to put these new competencies to work in the classroom (Floyd, 2003). "Technology is a critical part of every industry, and students must know how to use it effectively" (Harvey, 2004, p. 73). "Web-based courses also more easily fit into busy schedules when time is limited due to job and family responsibilities than do traditional courses" (Kubala, 2000, p. 338). Mastery of the new technologies benefits both faculty and learners through improved student-centered instruction (Ennis-Cole & Lawhon 2004; Zeszotarski, 2000).

"Even as technology use and application advance at an almost logarithmic pace, many of the issues related to technology use remain remarkably constant. These include properly trained staff, adequate equipment, ongoing funding, and successful integration of technology in order to maximize learning" (AL-Bataineh & Brooks, 2003, p. 473). While AL-Bataineh and Brooks concede that "technology offers educators one of the most powerful allies impacting how education is delivered and supplemented" (p. 483), they warn that the ultimate success of our schools still remains in training and supporting quality, irreplaceable faculty.

## FACULTY PROFESSIONAL DEVELOPMENT

Community college faculty represent almost one-third of the American professorate and teach nearly forty percent of all college students and almost fifty percent of all first-time freshmen (Prager, 2003). "With teaching at the heart of the enterprise, faculty are the key determinants in the success of the community college" (Wallin, 2003, p. 317). "There is an acute need to prepare new faculty and staff for the realities of work in the community college and build their commitment to the unique educational mission of [these] institutions" (Milliron & de los Santos, 2004, p. 113). Lawrenz, Keiser, and Lavoie (2003) point out, however, that many community college faculty may receive few opportunities for professional development and little financial support to participate in it.

In the community college, faculty need professional development to accommodate a changing economy, new technology, and an increasingly diverse student body (McKinney, 2004; Wallin, 2002) because "the faculty—their training, expertise, professionalism, attitudes—set the tone and the reputation of a college" (Wallin, 2003, p. 317). Professional development experiences, which target faculty as learners, have the potential to serve as catalysts for creating agents of major institutional change (Rouseff-Baker, 2002) and a cadre of scholars, who are reflective practitioners. "Faculty development can be viewed as the improvement of instruction in ways that benefit both the faculty member and the student" (Wallin, 2003, p. 319).

To bring faculty in closer working relationship with one another and to contribute to the enhancement of the professorate as a whole, Outcalt (2002) recommends the use of professional development programs focused on authenticating connections between teaching, research, and scholarship. Haworth and Wilkin (2004) remark that too few, if any, national programs exist that focus on preparing future community college faculty. Structured professional development experiences that enhance faculty knowledge and skills in three interrelated areas—information literacy, information technology, and the scholarship of teaching and learning—are timely for these faculty.

In a setting that is increasingly preferred by first-time-in-college students, faculty who are competent in and model the above skills can do much to demonstrate achievement of learning outcomes for a diverse student population. Murray (2002) points out, however, that successful faculty development programs must have administrative support; must be formalized, structured, and goal-directed; and must be valued by administrators.

## UNIVERSITY OF CENTRAL FLORIDA'S INNOVATIVE PROFESSIONAL DEVELOPMENT OPPORTUNITY

The University of Central Florida has provided strong administrative leadership and support for distributed learning, thereby avoiding and disavowing a one-size-fits-all format for teaching and learning. Today, the university is a leader in the use of digital media in instruction and is also recognized as an educational leader in distance education. Since 1996, the University of Central Florida has been conducting online graduate courses for community college personnel in Florida. Its Graduate Certificate for Community College Education, a fully Web-based professional development opportunity for practitioners, consists of five courses (Table 1).

**Table 1**
**University of Central Florida's**
**Online Professional Development Program**

| Course Prefix | Course Name and Description |
|---|---|
| **EDH 6053** | **The Community College in America.** Examines the history, philosophy, goals, and mission of the community college. |
| **EDH 6061** | **Contemporary Problems in Community Colleges.** Analyzes the critical issues facing community colleges today and in the near future. |
| **EDH 6204** | **Community College Organization, Admin. and Supervision.** Offers an analysis of the organizational structure and administrative functions of the community college as they relate to instruction and curriculum. |
| **EDH 6215** | **Community College Curriculum.** Examines the background, development, function, and goals of the curriculum of the community college. |
| **EDH 6305** | **Teaching and Learning in the Community College.** Focuses on the dynamics of teaching and learning in the community college setting. |

In this "Knowledge Era," Sherer, Shea, and Kristensen (2003) suggest that "faculty need an active, connected community to help filter the overwhelming availability of information, understand what they find, and use it appropriately" (p. 184). These authors contend that creating a vehicle—an online faculty learning community—to expand knowledge and learning opportunities for faculty, can enhance professional effectiveness in teaching and learning.

Through enrollment in the University of Central Florida's Graduate Certificate in Community College Education, community college practitioners participate in a structured professional development opportunity. The curriculum engages community college faculty, as well as other practitioners, as learners in an instructional setting in which they integrate information literacy, information technology, and the scholarship of teaching and learning. Upon completing one or more courses in this curriculum, practitioners are expected to do the following:

- Demonstrate competency in accessing online databases and in retrieving and evaluating peer-reviewed scholarly articles and publications through University of Central Florida and other library resources (Information Literacy)

- Demonstrate research and computer skills (Information Technology)

- Identify and develop, in the form of a scholarly paper, a researchable topic pertaining to the community college (The Scholarship of Teaching & Learning).

## SUMMARY AND CONCLUSIONS

The research and scholarship on teaching and learning in the community college continue to exist as developing areas. Regarding the demographics of those who write about this institution, Townsend, Bragg and Kinnick (2003) report that the majority of published articles are written by men and by individuals working at universities. These findings were based on a review of articles published in three national peer-reviewed journals devoted to research on this arena (the Community College Journal of Research and Practice, the Journal of Applied Research in the Community College, and the Community College Review) and two other publishing outlets, which are more practitioner-oriented (the Community College Journal and the New Directions for Community Colleges monograph series).

Faculty, who play a key role in the daily goings-on of instruction in the academic setting, have rich voices that can add much to the research dialogue. By incorporating the scholarship of teaching and learning in their classrooms, faculty may contribute substantive real-world empirical data and research findings to the national discourse on teaching and learning, while concurrently providing best practice instruction to students.

Schuetz (2002) identified "maintaining the educated workforce needed to meet the increasingly complex needs of the students and institutions" (paragraph 2) as a key and emerging challenge for community colleges. As twenty-first century workers, community college students are expected to cooperate and collaborate, exhibit critical thinking and problem-solving skills and demonstrate competence in basic information and technological literacy.

How teachers teach is often in direct response to how they learned (Brookfield, 2002). As a direct consequent of a variety of educational delivery mechanisms, faculty can no longer teach as they were taught, as new teaching and learning environments necessitate new teaching and learning strategies. To ensure frequent and repeated opportunities for learners to acquire and practice information literacy and technology skills, faculty must be willing to learn and model these skills in their classrooms. In that regard, effective teaching, directed toward improved student learning, is tantamount to establishing a professorate which operates with currency and competency on the frontline of instructional excellence.

With pending retirements and the need for replacements among faculty, an opportunity exists to create a new community of scholars. They must promote reform in curriculum and instruction through a variety of methods and techniques for facilitating disciplined and informed inquiry. Moreover, this community must enhance self- and student-content knowledge in information literacy, information technology, and the scholarship of teaching and learning for community college students. Through modeling the effective integration of information literacy, information technology and the scholarship of teaching and learning in their classrooms, this professorate is uniquely positioned to impact a large proportion of students in higher education who need these skills to succeed in contemporary learning and workplace environments.

If the great majority of community college faculty believe that teaching helps students make passionate connections to learning (O'Banion, 1997, p. 28), then the time has come to connect the dots between information literacy, information technology, and the scholarship of teaching and learning. In doing so, community college faculty honor and serve their most valued constituency—students—who deserve the best that the faculty's ongoing scholarship can provide (Sperling, 2003).

## REFERENCES

AL-Bataineh, A., & Brooks, L. (2003). Challenges, advantages, and disadvantages of instructional technology in the community college classroom. *Community College Journal of Research and Practice, 27*(6), 473-84.

Boyer, E. L. (1990*). Scholarship reconsidered: Priorities of the professoriate.* San Francisco: Jossey-Bass.

Brookfield, S. D. (2002). Using the lenses of critically reflective teaching in the community college classroom. *New Directions for Community Colleges, 118,* 31-38.

Cooley, N., & Johnstone, M. (2001). Professional development: The single most important IT challenge in the United States. *Journal of Faculty Development, 18*(1), 35-47.

Ennis-Cole, D. L., & Lawhon, T. (2004). Teaching, technology and support in the new millennium: A guide for new community college teachers. *Community College Journal of Research and Practice, 28*(7), 583-592.

Ereegovac, Z., & Yamasaki, E. (1998). *Information literacy: Search strategies, tools & resources.* Retrieved November 3, 2004 from    http://www.gseis.ucla.edu/ccs/digests/dig9808.html).

Floyd, D. L. (2003). Distance learning in community colleges: Leadership challenges for change and development. *Community College Journal of Research and Practice, 27*(4), 337-347.

Glassick, C. E., Huber, M. T., & Maeroff, G. I. (1997). *Scholarship assessed: Evaluation of the professoriate.* San Francisco: Jossey-Bass.

Harvey, S. (2004). Bridging the digital divide: How technology can change higher education delivery for high school students. *Community College Journal of Research and Practice, 28*(1), 73-74.

Haworth, J. G., & Wilkin, D. (2004). Community college learning and teaching (CCLT): A preparing future faculty program intentionally focused on the community college context. *Community College Journal of Research and Practice, 28*(1), 51-52.

Kasowitz-Scheer, A., & Pasqualoni, M. (2002). *Information literacy instruction in higher education: Trends and issues.* Retrieved October 29, 2004 from http://www.ericdigests.org/2003-1/information.htm.

King, K. P. (2001). Professors' transforming perspectives of teaching and learning while using technology. *Journal of Faculty Development, 18*(1), 27-34.

Kubala, T. (2000). Teaching community college faculty members on the Internet. *College Journal of Research and Practice, 24*(5), 331-339.

Lawrenz, F., Keiser, N., & Lavoie, B. (2003). Sustaining innovation in technological education. *Community College Review, 30(*4), 47-63.

Levinson, D. L. (2003). Introduction to faculty scholarship in community colleges. *Community College Journal of Research and Practice, 27*(7), 575-578.

Lyons, R., McIntosh, M., & Kysilka, M. (2002). *Teaching college in an age of accountability.* Upper Saddle River, NJ: Pearson Education.

McKinney, K. (2004). The scholarship of teaching and learning: Past lessons, current challenges, and future visions. In C. M. Wehlburg & S. Chadwick-Blossey (Eds.), *To improve the academy,* 22 (pp. 3-19). Bolton, MA: Anker.

Miller, M. T., & Pope, M. L. (2003). Integrating technology into new student orientation programs at community colleges. *Community College Journal of Research and Practice, 27*(1), 14-23.

Milliron, M. D, & de los Santos, G. E. (2004). Making the most of community colleges on the road ahead. *Community College Journal of Research and Practice, 28*(2), 105-122.

Murray, J. P. (2002). The current state of faculty development in two-year colleges. *New Directions for Community Colleges, 118,* 89-97.

O'Banion, T. (1997). *A learning college for the 21$^{st}$ century.* Phoenix: American Council on Education & The Oryx Press.

Outcalt, C. L. (2002). Toward a professionalized community college professorate. *New Directions for Community Colleges, 118,* 109-115.

Pemberton, F. L. N. (2001). Distance education: The soundness and excitement it brings to knowledge acquisition. *The Journal of Faculty Development, 18*(1), 15-18.

Prager, C. (2003). Scholarship matters. *Community College Journal of Research and Practice, 27*(7), 579-92.

Profeta, P., & Kendrick, M. (2002). Information literacy skills of community college freshmen. *Visions: The Journal of Applied Research for the Florida Association of Community Colleges, 3*(1), 35-41.

Rouseff-Baker, F. (2002). Leading change through faculty development. *New Directions for Community Colleges, 120,* 35-42.

Schuetz, P. (2002). *Emerging challenges for community colleges.* Retrieved November 26, 2004 from http://www.gseis.ucla.edu/ccs/digests/dig0207.htm).

Sherer, P., Shea, T., & Kristensen, E. (2003). Online communities of practice: A catalyst for faculty development. *Innovative Higher Education, 27*(3), 183-194.

Sophos, P. (2003). Information literacy at community colleges. *Community College Journal of Research and Practice, 27*(8), 735-739.

Southern Association of Colleges and Schools. (1996). *Criteria for accreditation.* Decatur, GA: Author.

Sperling, C. B. (2003). How community colleges understand the scholarship of teaching and learning. *Community College Journal of Research and Practice, 27*(7), 593-601.

Townsend, B. K., Bragg, D., & Kinnick, M. (2003). Who writes the most about community colleges? An analysis of selected academic and practitioner-oriented journals. *Community College Journal of Research and Practice, 27*(1), 41-49.

Wallin, D. L. (2002). Faculty professional development: Building a world of learners. *Community College Journal, 72*(5), 32-35.

Wallin, D. L. (2003). Motivation and faculty development: A three-state study of presidential perceptions of faculty professional development needs. *Community College Journal of Research and Practice, 27*(4), 317-335.

Warren, J. (2003). Changing community and technical college curricula to a learning outcomes approach. *Community College Journal of Research and Practice, 27*(8), 721-730.

Wilson, C. D., Miles, C. L., Baker, R. L., & Schoenberger, R. L. (2000). *Learning outcomes for the twenty-first century: Report of a community college study.* Mission Viejo, CA: League for Innovation in the Community College.

Zeszotarski, P. (2000). *Computer literacy for community college students.* Retrieved November 3, 2004 from http://www.gseis.ucla.edu/ccs/digests/dig0001.html.

**Note.** The author wishes to acknowledge the editorial assistance provided by Iris Rose Hart, Santa Fe Community College, whose knowledge and skill greatly improved the manuscript.

# THE INTERACTIVE ART

# OF CRITICAL THINKING

**Barclay Hudson**
*Fielding Graduate Institute*

## INTRODUCTION

This paper looks at critical thinking as one of education's highest arts. It begins with the definition of "critical thinking" offered by the American Philosophical Association's Delphi Report (American Philosophical Association, 1990), but finds a surprising gap in that definition—namely, the lack of any reference to interactive aspects. To compensate, this paper provides a tour of six other versions of critical thinking that give more emphasis to dialogue and interaction. The concluding section of the paper offers a handful of collaborative critical thinking tools for classroom and online use.

### Baseline Definition of Critical Thinking:
### The Delphi Report

Definitions of critical thinking abound (Van Gelder, 2004), along with a range of instruments to measure critical thinking competences (Facione & Giancarlo, 2000; Watson & Glaser, 1990). In 1987 the American Philosophical Association brought together 46 critical thinking experts to come up with a "consensus definition" (American Philosophical Association, 1990).

It's not too surprising that the Delphi Report omitted collaboration as an element of critical thinking. Traditionally, education has emphasized "excellence" with an implied focus on gifted students and outstanding teachers (or perhaps the good fortune to live in Garrison Keeler's legendary community of Lake Woebegone, where "every student is above average"). "Excellence" means personal achievement, and standing out from the pack, and critical thinking revolves around a somewhat self-centered, cerebral, even elitist exercise.

As might be expected from a large committee of academics seeking consensus, the Delphi definition is somewhat general, but also broad ranging. Even so, there's no mention of critical thinking as a collaborative, interactive process—a point to keep in mind while reading the Delphi definition that follows. "We understand critical thinking to be purposeful, self-regulatory judgment that results in interpretation, analysis, evaluation, and inference, as well as explanation of the evidential, conceptual, methodological, criteriological, or contextual considerations upon which that judgment is based" (American Philosophical Association, 1990, p. 2).

The Delphi definition continues in this vein for another 140 words, with allusions to critical thinking as "a tool of inquiry ... a liberating force ... a powerful resource ... a self-rectifying human phenomenon" (p. 2). It describes the ideal critical thinker as "habitually inquisitive, well-informed, trustful of reason, open-minded, flexible, fair-minded...honest...prudent...clear...orderly...diligent ...reasonable...focused...persistent...rational..." (p. 2)— but still nothing is mentioned about collaborative skills.

Whatever its other merits, the Delphi Report stressed that critical thinking applies to education at all levels, noting that in the previous decade of the 1980s, "the movement to infuse the K-12 and post-secondary curricula with critical thinking (CT) had gained remarkable momentum." (American Philosophical Association, 1990, p. 1). One aim of the present paper is to bring the notion of critical thinking down to earth, making it more accessible to students of all ages, and to academics from different disciplines.

*Is a single definition of "critical thinking" possible?*  In its focus on personal intellectual prowess, the Delphi Report chose not to address a central theme of late 20th Century thinking, spelled out in the title of Berger & Luckmann's seminal book, "Social Construction of Reality" (1966). Because ideas are socially constructed, and because cultures, settings, and people differ, ideas and conclusions are never completely objective, but only valid within circles of "inter-subjective" verification. Critical thinking is important not just because information is missing or people are sloppy thinkers, but because different people bring different information and mindsets to bear.

Thus, one key premise of the post-modern perspective is that there is no "meta-narrative" that works for everyone, or has validity for every purpose. Knowledge is relational—it gains meaning through its specific applications for a particular group. By logical extension, there can be no "standard" definition of critical thinking. In fact, consensus on a definition is almost an oxymoron, as the whole point of critical thinking is to call into question conventional wisdoms—including, of course, the convened wisdom of the 46 Delphi experts.

At least that's one alternative possible version of critical thinking, different from Delphi's. And there are other versions, too—the subject of the tour about to commence. There are two things to keep in mind. First, the tour both assumes and reinforces the idea that it is possible to follow diverse paths. Consensus may be one basis for establishing validity, but it can also impose shackles on thinking beyond conventional, committee-like thinking. Secondly, in moving beyond the Delphi definition, there is an unavoidable need to deal with critical thinking as a social, or relational art, where ideas aren't simply cards in a game of solitaire, but elements in a process of social negotiation. Ideas emerge and become validated on the basis of evolving relationships among people in dialogue, and not just from the solving of intellectual puzzles. Gödel's "incompleteness theorem" demonstrates that even in mathematics, fundamental axioms are not based on realities derived from an "objective" knowledge of the universe, but are formed out of human neuro-linguistic structures (Levin, 2002, p. 209) built out of human forms of communication and social relationships. In the same way, critical thinking is a social and interactive endeavor, not just a personal skill.

## SEVEN PERSPECTIVES ON CRITICAL THINKING

Table 1 summarizes seven different traditions of critical thinking, starting with the baseline Delphi definition, and moving on to six other approaches that give more weight to interactive dialogue. These approaches somewhat overlap, but occasionally present stark contrasts. Each has classroom applications, and each can make use of a variety of interactive inquiry methods, described in the final section of this paper.

**Table 1**
**Critical Thinking — Seven Perspectives**

| | Critical Thinking Perspective | A Sample of Authors |
|---|---|---|
| 1 | Critical Thinking Skills (individual skills) (Cognitive capacity, logic, rhetoric, mental models, statistics; scientific methods) | Campbell (1969) APA Delphi Report (American Philosophical Association, 1990) Herrmann (1996) Popper (1950) |

| 2 | Critical Thinking as Dialogue (Group skills) | Argyris (1999) Bohm (1996) Isaacs (1999) Johnson (1998) |
|---|---|---|
| 3 | CAD—The Dialectic of Critical Appreciation | De Bono (1971, 1985); Hudson (2002, 2003, 2004) Millar (2004) |
| 4 | Critical Thinking Epistemologies —Ways of knowing (Post-modernism) | Argyris (1999) Berger & Luckmann (1966) Gardner (1983) Korzybski (1948) Morgan (1986, 1997) Senge (1990) |
| 5 | Critical Thinking Language and Story-Telling (hegemony, controlling narratives | Bahktin (1981, 1984) Boje, Luhman & Baack (1999) Jencks & Riesman (1969) Lawrence & Phillips (1998) |
| 6 | Critical Theory (critical consciousness) | Ellul (1964) Diduck (1999) Harrington (1962) Roszak (1992), |
| 7 | Critical Thinking Praxis | Freire (1981), Horton (1998) Fisher, Rooke & Torbert (2000) Gagliardi (1999) Revans (1980) |

## Critical Thinking as Individual Skill-Set— The Delphi Baseline Definition

The skills emphasized in the Delphi Report (1990) bring into play cognitive capacity, logic, rhetoric and mental models. By stretching this definition, it might also include teachers' recognition of individual differences in learning and thinking. Examples might include Herrmann's "four-quadrant brain model" of thinking preferences (1996), Conant's "two modes of thought" (1964), and Gardner's notion of "multiple intelligences" (1993).

Also relevant are skills of logic and inference that come with statistical thinking—not the calculations themselves, but the standard cautions about drawing generalizations from limited data (Campbell, 1969). In a broader sense, critical thinking disciplines are reflected in the basic tenet of scientific investigation, especially in the concepts of putting ideas to empirical test and focusing attention on ideas that can be verified or falsified by experiment (Popper, 1950).

## Critical Thinking As Dialogue—Interactive Learning

Critical thinking is rarely a solitary endeavor. Some would even argue that the very basis of thinking is rooted in dialogue: statements evolve in response to others' ideas, and are framed in anticipation of others' reactions. Bakhtin (1981) goes so far as to say that language, social relationships, and even consciousness, are based on "dialogic" processes (Bakhtin, 1984, p. 293).

Much has been written on the practice of dialogue (Bohm, 1966; Rogers & Roethlisberger, 1952). "Dialogue analysis" has emerged as a field of its own, beginning in the 1970s, drawing on ethnographics, linguistics, psychology, logic, sociology, philosophy, and even artificial intelligence (Schwitalla, 1994). Johnson (1998) makes the point that creative and effective dialogue, especially in the context of groups and organizations, calls on a combination of interpersonal and even artistic skills, including some specific, powerful techniques that can be directly imported from improv theatre—using guidelines such as, "no wimping," "make the other guy look good," "see the world with big eyes," and so on.

## Critical Thinking As Dialectic— The Confrontation/Appreciation Balance

A key problem for critical thinking within a group is the application of criticism while maintaining a tone of appreciative inquiry and mutual respect (Millar 2004). Students and teachers are most familiar with critical thinking in the form of personal feedback, where "criticism" usually ends up being taken very personally. The very word "critical" has overtones of skepticism and intimidation. Especially in online forums, written criticism can be harsh when not moderated by voice inflections or gestures. The result can be a retreat from deep engagement into shallow politeness (Hudson 2002).

What's needed then is a fine balance—a dialectic— between critique and "appreciative inquiry" (Cooperrider & Srivastva, 1987; Millar 2004). A "dialectic" is difficult to manage, because it involves natural polarities, sometimes resolved by creative evolution toward a symbiotic amalgam of ideas (thesis and antithesis leading to synthesis), but sometimes creating oscillations between emphasis on one or another end of the polarity (Johnson 1992). In the case of critical dialogue, the dialectic between criticism and mutual support is heavily dependent on an initial phase of trust building, prior to engagement in skeptical or confrontational critical thinking engagement on the issues themselves (Hudson, 2002, 2003, 2004).

**Critical Thinking Epistemologies—**
**Interplay Among Different Ways of Knowing**

Epistemology addresses the question, *How do we really know what we think we know?* This form of critical thinking involves use of different ways of "knowing," recognizing that every thought is a mental construct filtered through several layers of language, social beliefs, perceptual frame, and analytical method. Korzybski put it in a nutshell—"The map is not the territory" (1948, p. 59).

One way to critically evaluate alternative frames of understanding is through analysis of metaphors, to systematically examine the validity and limits of mental models. Some authors argue that metaphors are the only way we can ever know things—because we can perceive something only as higher-level class of things already understood. Thus, organizational behaviors (for example) can be critically analyzed by systematically comparing alternative metaphors to see which best fits the phenomena being observed—organizations seen as organisms, or as well-oiled machines, as brains, as cultures, as psychic prisons, and so on (Morgan, 1986, 1997).

In talking about "learning organizations," Chris Argyris (1999) and Peter Senge (1990) describe specific disciplines for reflective or "double-loop" learning, which apply to the questioning of basic assumptions regarding the problem formulation and search for solutions. These disciplines involve social skills as much as mental skills. But they also involve a persistent unwillingness to take things for granted, which can become somewhat annoying —as any parent knows when a child keeps asking, again and again, the simple question, *Why?*

In most classrooms, not much room is given for this line of critical thinking, given the objectives and boundaries of prepared lesson plans. Training is as more about learning accepted truths than questioning of those basic assumptions, and problem-solving is designed around questions with known answers and a fixed set of steps from pre-determined problem to its approved solution, within the teacher's domain of expertise.  But one way to tell if a classroom is engaging in critical thinking is see if it allows thinking to go beyond the expected, calling for teachers with the courage to invite such questions that can only be answered, *Hmmm, I don't know.  Let's see if we can figure it out.*

## Critical Thinking as Language Deconstruction and Story-Telling

Mashoed Bailie identifies "critical communication scholarship" as a distinct form of dialogic inquiry, in which institutions and human relationships are examined in terms of "history, power, and struggle" (Bailie, 1995, p. 33). Here, the goal is to emancipate language through greater diversity of voices and through experience-based story telling that can challenge the abstractions of conventional beliefs or academic language.  Taking an inter-disciplinary perspective, Weigard (1994, p. 29-30) concludes that dialogue becomes especially interesting and fruitful when there is a switch in the implicit rules, a rupture in habitual assumptions, through the introduction of new voices bringing new "modalities" such as irony, pathos, humor, and exaggeration, or taking "time out to speak off the record."

Academic social criticism speaks of "discursive structures" and the "hegemony of dominant stories." (Boje, Luhman & Baack, 1999; Lawrence & Phillips, 1998).   In plainer English, this means that people tend to be drawn into kinds of discussion ruled by hidden assumptions, special vocabularies, and implicit rules of courtesy or attack. (Cilliers 1998; Lawrence & Phillips, 1998; Lyotard, 1984; Seidman, 1991).

In a famous study of professional training standards, Jenks & Riesman (1969) looked at the ways professional groups (teachers, doctors, lawyers, the military) gained the credentials of expertise, especially when dealing with people outside their own discipline. The study found two main devices forming the cornerstones of professional training—first, mastery of a specialized vocabulary, and second, "docility" of the uninitiated before the assumptions of the trade. In short, people trust their doctor because he/she uses Latin words they don't understand, and because the medical profession has closed ranks in support of its shared beliefs.

## Critical Thinking As Critical Theory— Insistence on Historical Context

This tradition of critical thinking gives central attention to the deeper context of the dialogue—the cultural, political and economic framework that sets the stage for the discourse at hand. Here, the focus is a critique of social institutions, examined in terms of "history, power, and struggle" (Bailie, 1995, p. 33). Whereas the postmodern mindset addresses the general difficulty of achieving objective conclusions, "critical theory" insists on identifying specific historical conditions that determine fundamental issues and social problems.

An explicit goal of critical theory is consciousness-raising, both to identify shared problems and to question the self-serving solutions offered by others. As Paolo Freire's describes the role of education (1981), it is aimed at students' development of a capacity to perceive "social, political and economic contradictions, and to take action against the oppressive elements of reality" (p. 19). There is some very eloquent writing on the role of education in liberation from manifest oppression (Horton, 1998; Greenwood & Levin, 1998; Rahman, 1993). And this leads to the final version of critical thinking, which focuses on getting beyond words to action as the ultimate test of validity for interactive social thinking.

### Critical Thinking as Praxis—
### A Form of Knowing that Insists On Doing

The action basis of critical inquiry can be traced back to Francis Bacon's 17th Century insistence on empirical investigation and inductive science, challenging the a priori method of medieval scholasticism. More recently, we have social experimentation, ranging from controlled experiments like the Hawthorne plant studies on worker productivity, to social reforms and "action research" putting heavier emphasis on community participation and dialogue as integral to the research. The tradition of participatory action research includes early work by Kurt Lewin (Gold, 1999), Donald Schön (1983) and Chris Argyris (Argyris, Putnam & Smith, 1985). William Torbert's "Action Inquiry" is one of the latest and most compelling theories in this tradition.  As Bailie (1995) puts it, "awareness is not sufficient unless it engages the will to act" (p. 49).

Action research, or participatory action research, provides the framework of "action learning" as formulated in Revans' classic book by that name (1980).  Action learning encounters difficulty in a classroom setting, but Revans made some key observations that apply directly to school practices.  He pointed out that—unlike traditional education or training—it is intensely collaborative; it aims at personal development as well as problem-solving, it calls for humility, patience, and time for personal reflection. Most important, it involves not so much trading of information and skills with others, but "trading of confusions."

## SOME TOOLS FOR CRITICAL THINKING

This concluding section summarizes a few methods of critical thinking that can be applied in the classroom, but also beyond. In fact, the majority of these methods have their origin in places that have a conscious view of themselves as "learning organizations" (Argyris, 1999; Senge, 1990). In this sense, they would apply not just to groups of students working together, but groups of educators seeking to introduce critical thinking as an interactive art, playing a more central role in the curriculum.

### Appreciative Inquiry

In contrast to most critical inquiry (*What's the problem? Where's the gap between reality and the goal?*) appreciative inquiry starts by looking at what has actually worked in the past, emphasizing that most solutions already exist, and people have more power to solve their own problems than outsiders give credit for. Emphasis is on empowerment, action learning (Cooperrider & Srivastva, 1987, Revans, 1980), and grounded theory, in place of academic theories and solutions that primarily serve the interests of outside suppliers. Appreciative inquiry is important to critical thinking in two respects: 1) it helps balance the negative aspects of criticism, which makes people resist new ideas (Millar, 2004); and 2) as a process for evaluating and learning from past experience, it helps get beyond generalizations ("this is a good program, or a bad experience"), to look at more specific contingencies of success ("it's positive in these respects but not those; the program works under these conditions but not those.")

**Authoritarian Classroom**

This is the name of a classroom exercise that grew out of "radical pedagogy" from the 1970s, using a debate format to address controversial social issues, but with each student assigned a Pro and Con position. The original idea was to demonstrate student docility in acceptance of social expectations, following any assigned party line. The exercise was inspired in part by contemporary experiments of Stanley Milgram on obedience to authority, and Philip Zimbardo on behavior in simulated prisons (Bower, 2004; Slater, 2004).

However, teachers found the exercise unexpectedly liberating for participants: it demonstrated the power of most students to take on creative thinking through role-playing, to be resourceful in raising intelligent objections to conventional wisdom, to see the world through unfamiliar eyes and engage in critical dialogue without personal affront, using voices of adopted personas. Contrary to original expectations, the exercise showed that individuals could revel in the holding of contrarian opinions in the face of groupthink pressures from others in the debate.

**Compass**

Developed at UCLA (in the Graduate Program in Urban Planning during the 1970s), the Compass method drew somewhat on the "Authoritarian Classroom" process above, adding elements from the Rand Corporation's Policy Delphi technique—a process for systematic pooling of expert judgment (Hudson, 1981). "Compass" stands for "Compact Policy Assessment" and aims at getting critical judgments from a diverse pool of experts or stakeholders without bogging down in polarized debate. It starts by going around the room asking each person in turn for a brief opinion on a "pathfinder" proposal or hypothesis, or perhaps a program to be evaluated.  Answers are recorded under columns labeled Pro and Con, going around the room for as many rounds as new points are offered.

As the process continues, a third column is added, not limited to Pros and Cons, but contingencies of truth, ("Well, it depends on ..." — bringing critical thinking into play through closer attention to local factors, contingencies of success, and conceptual distinctions. A final phase of the Compass process (the whole thing takes less than an hour) is designed to provide a follow-up research agenda on critical unresolved issues. "Critical" points are identified in two short stages.

## De Bono's Six Thinking Hats

This approach has evolved through decades of use both in business and school settings. It is based on de Bono's earlier work on "lateral thinking" (1971), but puts critical thinking into a simple format. This format makes it easy for participants to recognize different mindsets that can be brought to problem-solving and to quickly adopt those mindsets, either individually within a group or (more typically), with the whole group putting on one color hat or another in sequence  (de Bono, 1985).  A brief look at the colors:

- **White hat**—calls for information known or needed

- **Red**—Feelings, hunches, intuition

- **Yellow**—values, benefits, why something might work

- **Black**—Devils' advocate, why something might not work

- **Green**—Creative possibilities

- **Blue**—Managing the thinking process (facilitation)

**Path Analysis**

This simply means bringing the visual thinking part of the brain into play through a process of doodling with boxes and arrows to consider multiple paths of causes and outcomes. In systematic testing of ideas, one typically starts with a hypothesis, "A causes B," but it's never quite that simple. The A-B path goes through C. Besides, a correlation found between A and B may actually be due to the effect of another external variable (D) on both the input and output side. And so on. Some people are especially adept at visual thinking, but even for the doodle-challenged, sketching causal paths raises important questions about what the variety of factors involved, both within and outside the (assumed) main primary path of causation.

Some social science textbooks use the term "path analysis" in connection with statistical methods, but its greatest value is probably in the service of critically thinking about the variety of factors that impact any outcome and making considered choices about what variables to include or leave out of the research model. Once one's head is buried in the numbers, it's usually too late to re-draw the boundaries of the study. But using "path analysis" in a purely visual form of boxes and arrows provides a very accessible medium for people to work interactively, drawing on different expertise to argue the strength or weakness of different causal arrows in a graphic diagram.

## SCAMPER

This acronym stands for an assortment of tools for "lateral thinking" (de Bono, 1985), comprising *Substitute, Combine, Adapt, Modify, Magnify, Eliminate, Reverse* (McKenzie, 1998). It provides a method for looking at issues, hypotheses and situations in new ways. For example, if the initial hypothesis says something kind of obvious and insipid, like "Rewards boost performance," that statement can be turned on its head to ask *What if rewards actually get in the way of performance?* Is there a grain of truth there? Perhaps. In fact, there's some evidence that extrinsic rewards may tend to preempt the intrinsic reward of meaningful work (Lane, 1991).

### Visual I Ching

This is a purely graphic and intuitive way of depicting situations and issues. Participants are asked to consider a particular issue, and then take a few days to collect photos, sketches, or artwork that address the issue purely through graphic representation.

On reconvening, everyone posts their gathered material on the walls of a room. It is important at this stage that no one speaks. Still in a silent mode, everyone then considers the graphics that others have provided, considering the resonance or disconnect among different images. Again wordlessly, each person takes a half-dozen pins or stickies (a distinct color for each person), and puts those on the graphics that seem to best capture the issue presented at the outset.

In this process, people begin to see a clustering of pins—not a consensus, but different patterns of connection among the images that have "spoken" most powerfully to people, and define—in a completely non-verbal way—a particular mindset for seeing the issue. As a format for critical thinking, the Visual I Ching provides a fresh way of seeing relationships, allowing both clustering and differentiation among points of view, without the usual assumption that there is a right or wrong interpretation.

## CONCLUSIONS

The Delphi Report mentioned the importance of critical thinking to democratic processes. What this paper has attempted to offer is a series of ways to "democratize" critical thinking itself, taking it from a somewhat elitist emphasis on personal intellectual excellence, to a more collaborative forum and shared endeavor. Critical thinking is not for the intellect alone, but needs to draw upon—and in the process to reinforce—the interactive dimensions of thinking and working together.

And paradoxically, critical thinking, in a democratic context, needs to not just acknowledge but encourage different formats of critical thinking, different mindsets, different techniques of analysis, different kinds of voices in dialogue—beyond the traditional languages of academic disciplines. Attempting a single definition of critical thinking may actually be the antithesis of democratically constructive critical thinking.

## REFERENCES

American Philosophical Association. (1990). *Critical thinking: A statement of expert consensus for purposes of educational assessment and instruction* (the Delphi Report, executive summary). (ERIC Document Reproduction Service No. ED315423).

Argyris, C. (1999). *On organizational learning* (2nd ed.). Malden, MA: Blackwell.

Argyres, C., Putnam, R., & Smith, D. M. (1985). *Action science: Concepts, methods, and skills for research and intervention.* San Francisco: Jossey-Bass.

Bailie, M. (1995). Critical communication pedagogy: Teaching and learning for democratic life. In M. Bailie & D. Winseck (Eds.), *Democratizing communication?* (pp. 33-56). Cresskill, NJ: Hampton Press.

Bakhtin, M. M. (1981). *The dialogic imagination* (M. Holquist, Ed.). Austin, TX: University of Texas Press.

Bakhtin, M. M. (1984). *Problems of Dostoevsky's poetics* (C. Emerson, Ed.). Minneapolis: University of Minnesota Press.

Berger, P. L., & Luckmann, T. (1966). *Social construction of reality; a treatise in the sociology of knowledge* (1st ed.). Garden City, N.Y., Doubleday.

Bohm, D. (1996*). On dialogue* (L. Nichol, Ed.). New York: Routledge.

Boje, D. M., Luhman, J. T., & Baack, D. E. (1999). Hegemonic stories and encounters between storytelling organizations. *Journal of Management Inquiry, 8*(4), 340-360.

Bower, B. (2004). To err is human. Influential research attracts a scathing critique. *Science News, 166*(Aug 12), 106-8.

Campbell, D. T. (1969). Reforms as experiments. *American Psychologist, 24*(4), 409-429.

Cilliers, P. (1998). *Complexity and postmodernism. Understanding complex systems.* New York: Routledge.

Conant, J. B. (1964). *Two modes of thought; my encounters with science and education.* New York: Trident Press.

Cooperrider, D. L., & Srivastva, S. (1987). Appreciative inquiry in organizational life. *Research in Organizational Change and Development, 1,* 129-164. Retrieved January 3, 2005 from www.appreciative-inquiry.org/AI-Life.htm.

De Bono, E. (1971). *New think.* New York: Avon Books.

De Bono, E. (1985). *Six thinking hats.* Middlesex, England.

Diduck, A. (1999). Critical education in resource and environmental management: Learning and empowerment for a sustainable future, *Journal of Environmental Management, 57*(2), 85-97.

Ellul, J. (1964). *The technological society.* New York: Vintage Books.

Facione, P., Facione, N, and Giancarlo, C (2000). *The California Critical Thinking Disposition Inventory.* Millbrae, CA: California Academic Press.

Fisher, D., Rooke, D., & Torbert, B. (2000). *Personal and organizational transformations through action inquiry.* Boston: Edge\Work Press.

Freire, P. (1981). *Pedagogy of the oppressed.* New York: Continuum.

Gagliardi, P. (1999). Theories empowering for action. *Journal of Management Inquiry 8*(2), 143-147.

Gardner, H. (1993*). Multiple intelligences: the theory in practice.* New York: Basic Books.

Gold, M. (Ed.) (1999). *The complete social scientist. A Kurt Lewin reader.* Washington, DC: American Psychological Association.

Greenwood, D. J., & Levin, M. (1998). *Introduction to action research: Social research for social change.* Thousand Oaks, CA: Sage Publications.

Harrington (1962). *The other America: Poverty in the United States.* New York: Macmillan.

Herrmann, N. (1996). The four-quadrant brain model of thinking preferences. In E. Lumsdaine & M. Lumsdaine (Eds.) *Creative problem solving.    Thinking skills for a changing world* (pp. 74-111). New York: McGraw Hill.

Horton, M., Kohl, J. & Kohl, H. (1998). *The long haul: An autobiography.*  New York: Teachers College Press, Columbia University.

Hudson, B. (1981). Compass: A portable methodology for communications planning. In East-West Communication Institute, *Planning methods.* Honolulu: Unesco, EWCI.

Hudson, B. (2002). Critical dialogue online: Personas, covenants and candlepower. In K. E. Rudestam & J. Schoenholtz-Read, (Eds.), *Handbook of online learning. Innovations in higher education and corporate training* (pp. 53-90). Thousand Oaks, CA: SAGE Publications.

Hudson, B. (2003). Teaching in the electronic classroom: Initiating, maintaining, re-energizing. In A.DiStefano, K. E. Rudestam, & R. J. Silverman (Eds.), *SAGE encyclopedia of distributed learning.* Thousand Oaks, CA: Sage Publications.

Hudson, B. (2004). Collaborative learning online: *The 80/20 principle and re-design of faculty roles.* Unpublished manuscript, Fielding Graduate Institute.

Isaacs, W. (1999). *Dialogue and the Art of thinking together: A pioneering approach to communicating in business and in life.* New York: Currency.

Jencks, C., & Riesman, D. (1969). *The academic revolution.* Chicago: University of Chicago Press.

Johnson, B. (1992). *Polarity management. Identifying and managing unsolvable problems.* Amherst, MA: HRD Press.

Johnson, D. (1998). *Blazing with an inner light: The power of not knowing what comes next.* Unpublished Master's Thesis, The Fielding Institute, Santa Barbara, CA..

Korzybski, A. (1948). *Science and sanity; an introduction to non-Aristotelian systems and general semantics* (3d ed.). Lakeville, CN: Institute of General Semantics.

Lane, R. E. (1991). *The market experience.* New York: Cambridge U. Press.

Lawrence, T. B., & Phillips, N. (1998). Commentary: Separating play and critique: Postmodern and critical perspectives on TQM/BPR. *Journal of Management Inquiry, 7*(2), 154-160.

Levin, J. (2002). *How the universe got its spots. Diary of a finite time in a finite space.* New York: Anchor Books.

Lyotard, J. F. (1984). *The postmodern condition: A report on knowledge.* Manchester: Manchester University Press.

McKenzie, J. (1998). Grazing the net: Raising a generation of free-range students. *Phi Delta Kappan, 80*(1), 26-31.

Millar, P. A. (2004). *Conflict-positive organizations: Appreciative inquiry benefits from constructive conflict.* Unpublished Master's Thesis, The Fielding Institute, Santa Barbara, CA.

Morgan, G. (1986). *Images of organization.* Newbury Park, CA: Sage Publications.

Morgan, G. (1997). *Imagin-i-zation—new mindsets for seeing, organizing, and managing.* Thousand Oaks, CA: SAGE Publications.

Popper, K. (1950). *The logic of scientific discovery.* New York, Basic Books.

Rahman, M. A. (1993). *People's self development: Perspectives on participatory action research.* Atlantic Highlands, NJ: Zed Books.

Revans, R. W. (1980). *Action learning—new techniques for management.* London: Blond & Briggs.

Rogers, C. R. & Roethlisberger, F. J. (1952). Barriers and gateways to communication. *Harvard Business Review, 30*(4), 28-34.

Roszak, T. (1992). *The voice of the earth.* New York: Simon & Schuster.

Schön, D. (1983). *The reflective practitioner: How professionals think in action.* New York: Basic Books.

Schwitalla, J. (1994). The concept of dialogue from an ethnographic point of view. In E. Weigard (Ed.), *Concepts of dialogue, considered from the perspectives of different disciplines* (pp. 15-35). Tubingen, Germany: Max Niemeyer Verlag.

Seidman, S. (1991). The end of sociological theory: The postmodern hope. *Sociological Theory, 9*(2), 131-146.

Senge, P. M. (1990). *The fifth discipline. The art & practice of the learning organization.* New York: Currency Doubleday.

Slater, L. (2004). *Opening Skinner's box. Great psychological experiments of the twentieth century.* New York: W. W. Norton.

Van Gelder, T. (2004). *Critical thinking on the Web.* Retrieved November 29, 2004 from http://www.austhink.org/critical/pages/definitions.html.

Watson, G., & Glaser, E. (1990). *Watson-Glaser Critical Thinking Appraisal.* Kent, England: the Psychological Corporation.

Weigard, E. (Ed.). (1994). *Concepts of dialogue, considered from the perspectives of different disciplines.* Tubingen, Germany: Max Niemeyer Verlag.

# A BLENDED COURSE

# ON FEATURE WRITING

# FOR NEWSPAPERS AND MAGAZINES

**Yanick Rice Lamb**
*Howard University*

## INTRODUCTION

This paper will discuss a successful approach in creatively blending the traditional with the interactive in teaching "Feature Writing for Newspapers and Magazines" at Howard University. In addition to textbooks and handouts, the course incorporates Power Point presentations, the online Blackboard system, storytelling, peer-to-peer learning, guest lectures, site visits, as well as individual and team assignments.

## BACKGROUND INFORMATION

Just as there are several points of entry on a newspaper or magazine page, journalism professors at Howard University try to provide several points of entry in education, keeping in mind that different students require different modes of learning in line with Benjamin Bloom's taxonomy of learning objectives (Vangelisti, Daly, & Friedrich, 1999). Since this generation is far more visual and technically savvy, Howard has developed a successful approach in creatively blending the traditional with the interactive in teaching "Feature Writing for Newspapers and Magazines." This approach makes use of Bloom's theories by using a variety of methods to enhance retention, comprehension, application, analysis, synthesis and evaluation. In addition to textbooks and handouts, for example, the course incorporates Power Point presentations, the online Blackboard system, storytelling, peer-to-peer learning, guest lectures, site visits, as well as individual and team assignments across media platforms.

As professors share their passion and perspective, they bring the textbook and theory alive. Faculty members at Howard understand the importance of "finding time for contemplation and for rethinking their instructional goals" (Vangelisti, et al., 1999, p. 15). They understand the stuff that good professors are made of—the ability to bridge academia and the professional realm; to provide an enriching educational experience that blends scholarship, practical experience, theory and cutting-edge techniques; to be at once engaging and challenging; and to motivate students to reach their full potential. It has helped many students in shaping their goals and in beginning to identify their place in the world.

Education may begin in the classroom, but it extends far beyond it. In addition to developing the intellectual skills of students, one purpose of higher education is to take society to higher and higher planes. Journalism professors must always keep this in mind to silence, once and for all, the lingering debate over the value of a journalism education. True, a person can become a fine journalist without a journalism degree, but having one can lessen the learning curve.

What professors offer students is only a piece of the puzzle. Students must be challenged to extend their learning, to stretch and to think about purpose over paychecks. In the Department of Journalism at Howard the faculty attempts to diffuse the notion that students are playing or practicing at being a journalist. The position taken is that they are all journalists who happen to be students, working in a newsroom that happens to be a classroom.

## APPLYING THEORY TO PRACTICE

Workbook exercises are kept to a minimum so that students can do the real work of journalism, not "make work." Students are pushed to use their critical-thinking skills, by going beyond the obvious and focusing a great deal on the "how" and "why." Jo Sprague of San Jose State University notes that "to survive in a changing world and to participate effectively  in a democratic society, students must be prepared to critically analyze and evaluate ideas" (Vangelisti et al, 1999, p. 17). "During their brief years in the formal educational system, students learn techniques of research, inquiry, and problem solving that they can apply to new topics throughout their lives." (Vangelisti, et al., 1999, p. 17).

At Howard, writers are coaxed out of their comfort zones by being required to conduct much of their reporting off campus and in the communities of the Washington metropolitan area. They are encouraged to massage their story ideas and source lists, so that they don't simply write run-of-the-mill stories. They interview journalists who share their "beats" or specialty areas. A student with an international beat, for example, compared notes with a Moscow correspondent for The Washington Post via e-mail. Final projects are typically planned across media platforms (print, Internet, radio and television) so that students are comfortable reporting and collaborating on multimedia stories in this era of growing media convergence in which the public receives news by any necessary means—24 hours a day, 7 days a week.

To learn from the best, students read on their own or aloud in class and then dissect the works. In addition to creative nonfiction and novels, they read Pulitzer Prize-winning features; winning entries in the National Magazine Awards that are featured in The Best of American Magazine Writing (Perennial Currents, 2004), compiled annually by the American Society of Magazine Editors; a similar book from the American Society of Newspaper Editors, Best of Newspaper Writing (Bonus Books, 2004); winning student entries from the Hearst features competition and the Society of Professional Journalists' "Mark of Excellence" competition.

## Determining What Works Best

Howard, like many universities and media companies, is on a quest to determine what works best. As Howard continues to develop its Converged Media Lab, it is cognizant of key recommendations from the Freedom Forum on journalism education programs (Medsger, 1996): "Prepare students to think creatively in words and visual elements, to know the old methods of research and writing, and to anticipate and experiment with new methods" (p. 68). At the same time, educators and students are reminded that they "should not lose sight of the main point of journalism—how to find and tell word and visual stories" (p. 68). As Ryan and Tankard point out, "good writers can write for any medium and any purpose using any format, for they have mastered the fundamentals, and those don't change—regardless of medium or purpose" (2005, p. xxii).

In light of the above, Howard is not attempting to create legions of "backpack journalists" who can shoot still and video images, write stories, broadcast them, and maybe even produce. Rather than create jacks of all trades who are masters at none, Howard is preserving its tradition of producing exceptionally talented journalists who value good writing and specialize in print, broadcast or online journalism—such as the Pulitzer Prize-winning reporter Isabel Wilkerson of The New York Times. The difference is that today's students will not only specialize, but they will also be open to experimenting or collaborating in a converged environment. The technological revolution in media challenges educators to rethink what and how they teach in favor of "flexible, integrated and innovative media courses and curricula" (Blanchard and Christ, 1993, p. 22) that incorporate "broad-based, cross-media, integrative models" (Blanchard & Christ, 1993, p. 22).

**An Example**

A highlight of the feature writing course is a multimedia project that pulls together students in various classes. This assignment is an engaging extension of the standard group projects—or what some students describe as the "dreaded" group project. It is designed to prepare students for working in teams in their future newsrooms, especially in converged newsrooms.

During spring semester of 2004, three classes worked on a first-time collaboration involving Howard University's two independent newspapers, The Hilltop and The District Chronicles, and BlackCollegeView.com, a student Internet site operated in the Department of Journalism's Converged Media Lab. Reporting teams in the feature writing class came up with packages on Brown v. the Board of Education. The copy editors edited them, researching the issue beforehand, and the designers created layouts. The stories ran within the same week and some were later published on Black College Wire, based at Florida A&M University, for national distribution.

In the previous class, one team created its own Web site in addition to writing a series of print articles and coming up with a plan to tell those stories on radio and television. In 2005, the goal is to include students who work on the "NewsVision" television program, photographers and a radio correspondent at Howard who produces audio for BlackCollegeView.com and Black College Wire. Such efforts are already in place for the various Capstone courses, which also include public relations and advertising students to mirror what media companies do in the real world.

## Using the Web

Blackboard is also a key component of interactivity in the feature writing course. The online system has been useful for Associated Press style and current events quizzes; the occasional cyber class; group projects; study groups; posting grades, assignments and syllabi; links to examples of excellence in feature writing; links to research for the Brown vs. Board of Education and other projects; announcements; guests chats; class discussions; and a central place where each student can share tips and/or summaries on various topics. All of these are methods recommended by authorities on online learning (Draves, 2002). Draves also notes that cognitive learning is enhanced online, because students can study material at their own pace and peak learning time. They can also focus on specific content, test themselves daily and acquire research data quickly.

## Using Professionals from the Community

In addition, members of Investigative Reporters and Editors visit to explain the uses of computer-assisted reporting in which databases are mined to enrich stories. Other visiting journalists have included a Washington correspondent who assisted students in covering a redistricting case and directed them to Internet resources via e-mail. Students later joined the reporter in federal court to cover a redistricting case on deadline while observing her in action. One class conducted a group interview of a

Howard alumna who made the transition from journalist to author, comparing notes on the differences and similarities in the resulting articles. Another got a reality check as a pair of married columnists shared how they balance their professional and personal lives—and how they deal with the wife's proclivity for making private details part of her public platform.

## More Experiential Learning

The experiential learning also includes pairing feature writing students with students in a copy editing class throughout the semester so that they learn the experience of working one-on-one. The reporters gain more guidance on their stories and develop a partnership with a specific editor. The editors learn the care and feeding of reporters, the use of a scalpel rather than a machete, and how to preserve the voice of a writer without injecting their own or over-editing.

## THE RESULTS

By the end of the semester, students have learned how to research, write and publish various types of articles, including profiles, news features, how-to articles, essays, reviews, service pieces, and special reports. They have a better grasp of long-form articles and the best techniques of narrative or literary journalism. And they have learned to shape and develop article ideas; analyze magazines and specific markets; and write effective query letters for local and national magazines.

After completing this course, students have been so motivated that they have formed an association called Cover 2 Cover, organized two national conferences on magazine publishing and coordinated a trip from Washington to New York to visit various magazines. In addition, many students have volunteered to assist in expanding the magazine curriculum and in developing a student magazine. These efforts have directly resulted in freelance assignments, internships, full-time employment and other networking opportunities. They have also enhanced ties with the Magazine Publishers of America, which co-sponsored the first conference; the American Society of Magazine Editors; and many publishing executives.

## SUMMARY AND CONCLUSIONS

The Howard experience is all part of preparing journalists of tomorrow to do their part in moving society to a higher plane. Journalism professors are fine-tuning students' critical-thinking skills, injecting them with a healthy dose of cynicism that is essential in deciphering news from hype, showing them how to extend learning outside of the classroom, helping them make early forays into newsrooms, and giving them a solid foundation in reporting as well as ethics, media law and other areas.

Faculty and students are also learning the importance of settling for nothing less than excellence in journalism; protecting the public trust and the public's right to know; giving voice to the voiceless; comforting the afflicted, and afflicting the comfortable. As one of the premier historically black colleges and universities, Howard also encourages students to be leaders of the global community by championing diversity and painting a full, fair and balanced portrait of the world.

Palmer notes that "good teachers join self and subject and students in the fabric of life" (1998, p. 11). "Good teachers possess a capacity for connectedness. They are able to weave a complex web of connection among themselves, their subjects, and their students so that students can learn to weave a world for themselves" (p. 11).

As journalism continues to evolve, educators can continue to be at the forefront in weaving students "into the fabric of community that learning, and living, require" (p. 11) as well as leading the media industry in directions in which it should go.

## REFERENCES

Blanchard, R. O., & Christ, W. G. (1993). *Media education and the liberal arts: A new blueprint for the new professionalism.* Mahwah, NJ: Lawrence Erlbaum Associates.

Bonus Books. (2004). Chicago: Author. www.bonus-books.com.

Draves, W. A. (2002). *Teaching online.* River Falls, WI: LERN Books.

Medsger, B. (1996). *Winds of change: Challenges confronting journalism education.* Arlington, VA: Freedom Forum.

Palmer, P. J. (1998). *The courage to teach: Exploring the inner landscape of a teacher's life.* San Francisco: Joss-Bass.

Perennial Currents. (2004). http://www.directtextbook.com/browse.php.

Ryan, M., & Tankard Jr., J. W. (2005). *Writing for print and digital media.* New York: McGraw-Hill.

Vangelisti, A. L., Daly, J. A., & Friedrich, G. W. (1999). *Teaching communication: Theory, research and methods.* Mahwah, NJ: Lawrence Erlbaum Associates.

# INSTRUCTOR PERSONALITIES

# AND TEACHING WITH COMPUTERS

**Claire Rundle**
*Regent University*

## INTRODUCTION

If someone says, "I'm just not a computer person," does that mean that person is being closed-minded? Or is there really such a thing as a computer personality? The literature provides interesting research on computer anxiety and on computer self-efficacy in teachers. However, very few studies have attempted to relate personality to willingness to use computers for instruction. Personality is known to affect a person's attitude toward divorce, religion, the media, and second-language learning, but hypotheses about personality and computer-related attitudes are not yet well developed (Francis, Katz & Evans, 1996).

At the dawn of the $21^{st}$ century, there was pressure on educators at all levels, including institutions of higher learning, to incorporate computer work into their curriculums. This new initiative was based on research that established computer skills as a leading indicator of academic achievement (U.S. Department of Education, 1996). President Clinton (1997) promised, during his second inaugural address, that the power of the information age would be within reach of everyone. A 10-year study, funded by Apple Computer, Inc., found that students in technology-rich learning environments not only performed well on standardized tests, but they also developed other competencies; for example, they—unlike students in traditional classes—were becoming independent learners and sharers of their knowledge (Jonassen, Peck, Wilson, & Pfeiffer(1998).

While policy makers were convinced that computer skills led to academic success for students, some teachers were reluctant to adopt computers for their teaching. According to the Office of Technology Assessment (1995), it was faculty who would play the decisive role in determining how successful technology would be in education. William A. Long (1989) maintained that the learning of new behaviors was related to an individual's personality. So, as the profession of college instructor changed, as new technology requirements and expectations were added, the question of how personality might relate to using computers needed to be explored.

## DESCRIPTION OF THE STUDY

Faculty in humanities-related subjects (N=84) at Edison College in Southwest Florida filled out two questionnaires: a personality test and a survey of their willingness to use computers for instruction. There were two main study questions:

- *What are the distributions of self-perceived personality Types and Traits, as measured by the Long/Dziuban Checklist (1998)?*

- *To what degree do instructors' self-reported Types and Traits relate to their Willingness scores?*

The personality test was the Long/Dziuban Checklist (1998) for Types and Traits (Tables 1 and 2). This instrument classifies personalities as either Aggressive or Passive, and within the two basic personalities, there are two sub-groups:  (1) Independent and  (2) Dependent, totaling four Types: 1) Aggressive Independent; 2) Aggressive Dependent; 3) Passive Independent; and 4) Passive Dependent. Faculty members selected the single type that best fit them.

**Table 1**
**The Long/Dziuban Checklist for Personality Types**
**(Check ONE that most describes you)**

| _____A | _____B |
|---|---|
| • Highly energized and action-oriented | • Lower energy level |
| • Little need for approval; unconcerned with pleasing others | • Little need for approval; unconcerned with pleasing others |
| • Puts thinking into immediate action | • Independent and strong-willed |
| • Very frank, speaks out freely | • Sometimes non-communicative |
| • Is truthful about feelings | • Prefers to work alone |
| • Has no problem confronting people | • May resist pressure from authority |
| | • Independent thinker |

| _____C | _____D |
|---|---|
| • Highly energized, and productive<br>• Strongly motivated by approval<br>• Sensitive to the wishes of others<br>• Translates energy to constructive tasks<br>• Deeply values close bonds with others<br>• Some difficulty dealing with direct confrontation<br>• Highly idealistic, setting lofty goals for themselves<br>• Fosters harmonious relationships | • Lower energy level<br>• Needs approval – Concerned with pleasing others<br>• Rarely shows anger or resentment<br>• Very sensitive to the feelings of others<br>• Very compliant and loyal<br>• Forms strong attachments<br>• Gives and thrives on affection |

**Table 2**
**The Long/Dziuban Checklist for Personality Traits (Check as many as apply to you)**

| _____Trait 1 | _____Trait 2 |
|---|---|
| • Thinks of all possibilities and<br>• contingencies before venturing into<br>• activities<br>• "What if" . . . person<br>• May see the negative side of things<br>• Unwilling to take risks | • Highly organized and methodical<br>• Strongly motivated to finish tasks<br>• Perfectionistic<br>• Tends to form habits<br>• Extremely diligent in work habits<br>• May be mildly ritualistic |

| _____Trait 3 | _____ Trait 4 |
|---|---|
| • Sometimes explosive and quick-tempered<br>• Sharp tongued<br>• Very frank<br>• May act without thinking | • Dramatic<br>• May have wide mood swings<br>• May overreact in some situations<br>• Can have emotional outbursts<br>• Creative thinker (rich imagination)<br>• Artistically inclined<br>• Devalues routine work |

A questionnaire was designed to reveal the instructors' "willingness" to use computers for instruction, based on their Efficacy, Attitude, and actual Usage. The instrument was derived from one developed by RAND researchers (Tschannen-Moran, Hoy & Hoy, 1998). It began with questions about prior training or experience an instructor may have had, factors which had been proven to affect computer use (Georgi & Crowe, 1998). The items then followed (table 3):

**Table 3**
**The Willingness Questionnaire**

*Please indicate which computer activities you use for instruction presently or would like to use in the future.*

| Instructional Activities | Do Now | Would Like To |
|---|---|---|
| 1.  Composing and editing essays with a word processing program . . . . . | ——— | ——— |
| 2.  Accessing information from electronic databases . . . . . . . | ——— | ——— |
| 3.  Differentiating between refereed electronic databases and the Web . . | ——— | ——— |
| 4.  Participating in online discussions . . | ——— | ——— |
| 5.  Creating PowerPoint presentations . | ——— | ——— |
| 6.  Interactive tutorials . . . . . . . | ——— | ——— |
| 7.  Course companion Web site . . . . . | ——— | ——— |
| 8.  Other computer instructional uses (please specify) _____ | ——— | ——— |

## FINDINGS

Of the 84 respondents, an overwhelming majority (81%) reported that their behavior was best described by Types A or C—the Aggressive—or high-energy—types. The most dominant combination of Type and Traits was Aggressive-Dependent and Compulsive (60%)—Tables 4 and 5.

**Table 4**
**Distribution of Personality Types**

| | |
|---|---|
| Type    A    –    Aggressive Independent – 24% | Type B – Passive Independent – 9.5% |
| Type C – Aggressive Dependent  –  57% | Type D – Passive Dependent – 9.5% |

**Table 5**
**Distribution of Traits within the Types**

| Traits: | Type A Aggressive-Independent | Type B Passive-Independent | Type C Aggressive-Dependent | Type D Passive-Dependent |
|---|---|---|---|---|
| Phobic | 35 % | 37 % | 30 % | 50 % |
| Compulsive | 40 % | 75 % | 60 % | 37% |
| Impulsive | 0% | 12.5 % | 10 % | 0 % |
| Hysteric | 50 % | 50 % | 32 % | 37.5 % |

There were no significant correlations between personality Types and the Efficacy, Attitude, and actual Usage scores, but two Traits did show significant correlations with Efficacy, Attitude, and Actual Usage scores—the Compulsive and the Hysteric Traits (Table 6).

**Table 6**
**Correlation Between Efficacy, Attitude, and Actual Usage (Willingness) Scores and Two of the Traits**

| | Compulsive | Hysteric |
|---|---|---|
| Pearson Correlation | -.33** | .24* |
| Sig. (2-tailed) | .002 | .032 |

Note:   **.01 level (2-tailed).
      *  .05 level (2-tailed).

## CONCLUSIONS

Based on the data collected, an overwhelming majority (81%) of Edison College faculty were classified as high-energy (Aggressive) individuals. Most of them (60%) appeared to be "people pleasers" (Dependent). Most claimed the Compulsive set of Traits, the set which correlated negatively with willingness to use computers for instruction. Nearly half claimed the Hysteric Trait (46%), indicating a possible willingness to use computers. Some claimed both.

Three characteristics of the Hysteric Trait set correspond with Impulsive behavior: 1) wide mood swings; 2) overreaction; and 3) emotional outbursts. These three characteristics were not prevalent among the faculty since only 10% claimed Impulsive traits. It may be concluded, therefore, that the great majority of Hysterics possessed the remaining four characteristics on the Hysteric list. These are: 1) dramatic; 2) creative-thinking; 3) artistically inclined; and 4) likely to devalue routine work. This conclusion could lead to understanding what kind of personality is likely to embrace computers for instructional purposes—Hysteric but not Impulsive! More research in this subject might help colleges to tailor their faculty workshops to personality traits.

## REFERENCES

Clinton, B. (1997). Second inaugural address of William J. Clinton January 20, 1997. *Presidential Studies Quarterly, 27*(Winter), 107-110.

Francis, L. J., Katz, Y. J., & Evans, T.E. (1996). The relationship between personality and attitudes toward computers: An investigation among female undergraduate students in Israel. *British Journal of Educational Technology, 27,* 164-70.

Georgi, D. & Crowe, J. (1998). Digital portfolios: A confluence of portfolio assessment and technology. *Teacher Education Quarterly, 25*(1), 73-84.

Jonassen, D. , Peck, K., Wilson, B., & Pfeiffer, W. (1998). *Learning with technology: A constructivist perspective.* Upper Saddle River, NJ: Prentice Hall.

Long, W. A. (1989). Personality and learning: 1988 John Wilson Memorial Address. *Focus on Learning Problems in Mathematics 11*(4), 1-16.

Long, W. A. & Dziuban, C. (1998). *The Long/Dziuban Checklist.* Unpublished manuscript.

Office of Technology Assessment. (1995). *Teachers and technology: Making the connection.* OTA-EHR-616. Washington, DC: U.S. Government Printing Office.

Tschannen-Moran, M., Hoy, A. W., & Hoy, W. K. (1998). Teacher efficacy: Its meaning and measure. *Review of Educational Research, 68*(2), 202-248.

U.S. Department of Education (1996). *Getting America's students ready for the 21$^{st}$ century: Meeting the technology literacy challenge.* Retrieved November, 2004 from www.fred.net/nhhs.html.

# TEACHING ACTIVITY-BASED INTRODUCTORY

# PHYSICS IN LARGE CLASSES:

# THE SCALE-UP PROJECT

**Jeffery M. Saul**
*University of Central Florida*
**Robert J. Beichner**
*North Carolina State University*

## INTRODUCTION

The Student-Centered Activities for Large Enrollment Undergraduate Programs (SCALE-UP) Project has established a highly collaborative, hands-on, computer-rich, interactive learning environment for large-enrollment courses. Class time is spent primarily on hands-on activities, simulations, and interesting questions as well as hypothesis-driven labs. Students sit in groups at round tables. Instructors circulate and work with teams and individuals, engaging them in Socratic-like dialogues. Rigorous evaluations of learning have been conducted in parallel with the curriculum development effort. The findings can be summarized as follows—ability to solve problems is improved, conceptual understanding is increased, attitudes are improved, failure rates are drastically reduced (especially for women and minorities), and performance in follow up physics and engineering classes is positively impacted

In this paper the studio-style classroom environment will be discussed as well as how its features promote the desired interactions. The results of a variety of assessments of student learning will also be presented.

## WORKSHOP/STUDIO-STYLE CLASSES

...I point to the following unwelcome truth: much as we might dislike the implications, research is showing that didactic exposition of abstract ideas and lines of reasoning (however engaging and lucid we might try to make them) to passive listeners yields pathetically thin results in learning and understanding–except in the very small percentage of students who are specially gifted in the field (Arons, 1990, p. vii).

Evidence supports the concept that students can learn more physics in classes where they interact with faculty, collaborate with peers on interesting tasks, and are actively involved with the material they are learning (Hake, 1998; Mazur, 1997; McDermott, 1991; Redish & Steinberg, 1999; van Huevelen, 1991). Research on learning and curriculum development has resulted in instructional materials that can correct many of the shortcomings of traditional physics instruction.

Careful study of research-based introductory curricula in small classes indicate that they can significantly improve students' conceptual understanding (Hake, 1998; Heller, Keith & Anderson, 1992; Law, 1991; Redish, Saul & Steinberg, 1997). However, introductory physics instructors with large classes who want to incorporate active learning into their classrooms must typically choose between: 1) hands-on activities (Beichner, et al., 1999) in small recitation or laboratory sections that supplement the lecture (McDermott, et al., 1998); and 2) interactive lecture activities for larger classes like Peer Instruction (Fagen, Couch, & Mazur, 2002; Mazur, 1997) and Interactive Lecture Demonstrations (Sokoloff & Thornton, 1997) that do not permit hands-on experiments and limit faculty interactions with individual groups.

Studio-style classes, where students work in teams observing and studying physical phenomena, offer faculty a third option.

## The SCALE-UP Model

SCALE-UP provides studio/workshop classes that replace the lecture/laboratory format with 4-6 hours of activity-based instruction per week in 2-hour blocks. This format has several advantages over the traditional lecture/laboratory format. Since the entire class is taught in the same room with the same students and instructors in each class, all activities, including laboratory experiments, can be arranged to build on one another in sequence for greater learning impact (Coleman, Holcomb, & Rigden, 1998) than when some activities are taught in small sections running parallel to the lecture course.

When a lab section is taught as a separate course, it is often either weeks or at best a few days ahead of or behind the lecture and for some students, the lab course is not even taken in the same term as the lecture. In addition, to better integrate lab experiments into the course, a studio format allows for a greater variety of hands-on activities including microcomputer-based laboratory and simulations since each student group can have access to a computer and lab equipment during any part of the course. Last but not least, in an interactive lecture, students can avoid instructors by hiding in the middle of the row, away from the aisles. In the studio format, instructors can freely circulate and interact with any group at any time.

Other examples of workshop/studio-style curricula (McDermott & Redish, 1999) include the Workshop Physics curriculum developed at Dickinson College (Laws, 1997) and the Studio Physics curricula at RPI (Wilson, 1994) and Cal Poly San Luis Obispo (Knight, 2000). These curricula have the advantages described above, but are difficult to implement at large research universities because of class size limitations. The SCALE-UP project is an effort to create studio classes that would be large enough to provide an effective, yet affordable alternative to large classes taught via the standard lecture/laboratory format.

As with the other research-based curricula described above, in SCALE-UP classes the students work through activities in small groups of 3-4 students each. However, in SCALE-UP classes, both the activities and the classroom have been modified for larger student/faculty ratios of 25-50 to 1, which permits class sizes of 50-120 students with 2-4 instructors (faculty & Teaching Assistants). Thus SCALE-UP makes it practical to offer activity-based classes with integrated hands-on labs even at schools like North Carolina State University and the University of Central Florida, where thousands of students are enrolled in the introductory physics classes each year.

## COOPERATIVE GROUPS OF STUDENTS

The SCALE-UP format takes advantage of cooperative learning techniques and helps students form learning communities which can make education at large universities seem much less impersonal, particularly for students taking mainly large introductory classes in their freshman and sophomore years. Interactions between students and with faculty are claimed to be the most important aspect of a successful college career (Astin, 1993).

There are many benefits to placing students into formal cooperative groups. Because they talk with each other, they are naturally more active (or interactive). Obviously, when an individual student reaches an impasse, they are stuck. Calling on teammates can provide additional resources and avenues to success. Seeing how others approach problems can be very valuable, especially for students whose performance is low. Also, by careful design of instruction, students can be placed into situations where they work at the upper levels of Bloom's taxonomy—synthesis and evaluation of each other's ideas. Perhaps most importantly, grouped students benefit from cognitive rehearsal: they learn more when they teach others.

Johnson, Johnson, & Smith (1991) present five required characteristics of successful group-based instruction. There has to be individual accountability, positive interdependence, opportunities for interaction, appropriate use of interpersonal skills, and regular self-assessment of group functioning. The authors have found that not incorporating all these aspects is a recipe for failure, at least as far as group functioning is concerned.

**Making Groups Work**

Several instructional methods have been incorporated to ensure each of the above characteristics is present. For example, there appear to be types of students who don't want to participate in groups. The better students often don't want to work with their peers because they believe they will be "slowed down" by the poorer students. (They don't recognize what they themselves gain while explaining concepts to others.) Because these students are many times motivated by grades, "teamsmanship points" are provided to each member of any group whose exam average is 80% or better.

Low-end students often don't want to participate in a group because they are lazy. Since they tend to avoid work, a mechanism is provided whereby they can be "fired" from their group for poor performance. In practice, this means they would have to do the entire group's work by themselves—highly undesirable to a student trying to avoid work. Having students write their own contracts helps students manage their own group operation.

Efforts are made to ensure heterogeneity within groups and homogeneity between them. At the beginning of the semester the students are ranked by an appropriate measure of their background (FCI pretest scores, grades from previous physics courses, GPA, etc.). Each group has one student from the top, middle, and bottom third of the class ranking. Each table is assigned one of the very best students and no female or minority students are by themselves. It's been found best in this project to create new groups every few weeks, typically after an exam. Waiting longer causes problems because of the strong friendships that tend to form in long-established groups, leading to reluctance to later group reshuffling. It does not appear to be as important to match female and minority students in the later groups.

## THE PHYSICAL LEARNING ENVIRONMENT

It's important to redesign the physical classroom environment to better promote active, collaborative learning. After experimenting with various shapes and sizes of tables, seven foot round tables with comfortable chairs placed around them are used in this project, which appears to facilitate communication. The 7-foot tables appear to be the best compromise between "elbow room" and closeness for conversation, although they are not an industry-standard size. (See Fig. 1a.). Each table seats three teams (called A, B, and C) of three students. The tables are numbered so a specific team can be identified (e.g. Group 4C), an entire table can be selected, the entire room can be divided in half by specifying even and odd table numbers, or the room can be split into thirds by calling on all the "A groups" to do one task while the "B groups" and "C groups" work on their own activities. Each individual student has their own nametag so that no one can be anonymous, even in a large classroom.

The instructor station (Fig. 1b) is a smaller table or podium that is placed near the center of the room. It is outfitted with a computer and video presentation system (basically a video camera mounted on a stand). Both of these devices are connected to ceiling-mounted projectors.

**Figure 1**

**a) Student Table;**
**b) Instructor Station;**
**c) Schematic Classroom Layout (Seats 99 Students)**

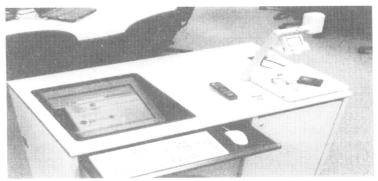

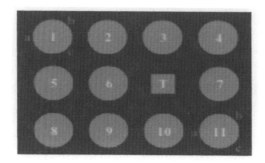

## Student Technology Resources

The number and placement of computers in the classroom was examined, and it was determined that one laptop computer per team was sufficient (for Web-based quizzes or tests, this number may need to be increased). In this situation laptops were preferred to desktop systems because of their smaller "footprint" and lower monitor height. It is also very helpful to tell students to close the lids of their computers when they are being distracted by the ever-present Internet and Instant Messenger.

Large white boards mounted on the walls (and/or smaller, portable group boards) have multiple benefits. Since students do their "thinking" on these public spaces the instructor can more easily see how groups are progressing during an activity. In addition, students can view/critique each other's boards while working or as a tool for presentation to the entire class. A whiteboard can be seen behind the table in Figure 1a.

A wireless microphone has also been found to be helpful when the instructor wants everyone's attention. The majority of class time is spent with the students working in groups as the instructor and assistant(s) circulate throughout the room. Getting students to look away from an engaging task is much easier if they don't know if the instructor trying to get their attention is across the room or right behind them!

## ENGAGING ACTIVITIES

A major advantage to having student groups working on activities is that it frees instructors from standing in the front of the room. A faculty member, graduate student, and if possible an undergraduate are sufficient to monitor the work of 99 students. Walking around the room and glancing at whiteboards provides considerable feedback to the teachers.

Progress is ensured by engaging students in semi-Socratic dialogs (Hake, 1992). However, a careful balance must be maintained between continually asking questions and students feeling like they will never hear an answer from the instructor. By strongly encouraging acceptable answers and providing end-of-activity summaries (by teachers and students), students feel they reach closure for a particular task. This must be done while not disparaging incorrect answers. Students need to take risks, so instructors must try to find something to praise, even as they carefully guide the students from a misunderstanding toward the desired goal.

For example, students displaying the classic "charge is consumed in a resistor" error can be asked questions about charge conservation to facilitate their accepting current as a circulation of charges. Then they can be helped to understand that it is energy that is "used up" in a resistor (in the sense that it is changed into heat) and that perhaps that concept is what they were thinking about originally. This type of interchange takes practice on the instructor's part and training of teaching assistants. It is especially important that teachers don't try to "show what they know" by simply telling students the right answer. This is truly a situation where the teacher is the guide at the side and not the sage on the stage. Nature is the authority, not the book or instructor.

## Lesson Plans

To relieve some of the burden from instructors, a large set of research-based lesson plans was created. In some cases these are entirely new materials, in others, existing curricula was modified.

For example, it was found that the effectiveness of the popular Washington Tutorials (McDermott, et al., 1998) suffers when used with 99 students at once. This is probably because the student/faculty ratio is much larger than the developers had in mind. These activities were modified and broken into 10 to 15 minute tasks that are delivered via the Web. Activities are pass-word protected so that students can't start them early; it's important that they interact with each other and the instructors while they are working.

*Keeping the Class Interesting.* To keep the class interesting, several different types of group activities were developed. *Tangibles* are short tasks where students make some sort of hands-on measurement or observation. Examples include determining the thickness of a single sheet of paper in their textbook (for practice with significant figures and estimating), calculating the number of excess charges on a piece of transparent tape after it is pulled up from the tabletop, determining the desired spacing of frets on a guitar, or estimating the amount of force needed to roll a racquetball along a circular arc.

*Ponderables* similarly require estimating or finding values from the Web, but there are no observations needed. Students are asked questions like: *Estimate the number of steps it takes to walk across the country,* or *How far does a bowling ball skid before its motion is purely rolling?* These questions are hard enough that students appreciate having their teammates available to help. They also evaluate the quality of other groups' efforts.

*Software.* Software is available for students to use as they grapple with difficult concepts. Simulation packages, spreadsheets, and concept-oriented programs are used extensively. Many are Java-based, like Physlets® (Christian & Belloni, 2001), and are delivered via the Web. An important aspect to realize is that the simulations are used to help students more thoroughly understand the real world and are not a substitute for hands-on experience.

*Labs.* substantial changes have been made to the labs students work on during the semester. Because it's not necessary to rely on labs to be the only place where students "do physics," it's possible to concentrate on other areas like uncertainties, hypothesis testing, and experimental design.

For example, one lab has them taking static measurements of a mass/spring system and then predicting what a graph of the oscillating vertical position of the mass would look like. Because students don't realize the spring's mass cannot be ignored in this particular situation, their predictions are wrong. They spend the rest of the time trying to isolate the problem and using software to model the spring as a series of small objects connected by stiffer springs.

*Problem Solving Protocol.* Students are provided with a problem solving protocol based on the work of Polya (1973). *GOAL* is a mnemonic for easy recall. *G* reminds students to carefully Gather information by looking for key phrases, getting a "big picture" view of the situation, estimating the final answer, etc. *O* stands for Organize and is where the problem is classified by the physics principles involved. A written plan of action and drawing help students clarify their thoughts (and assist instructors when they grade the solution). During the Analysis step (*A*), students carry out the calculations needed for a mathematical answer and then incorporate the numbers gathered initially. Finally, students must Learn ($L$) from their work. They check the answer for reasonableness, correct units, etc. They look at limiting cases to see if their algebraic result behaves properly. They also consider what they should have learned from this particular problem.

Without requiring this last step ($L$), students often write the final number down from their calculator and never give it a second thought. It's important for them to go through some of the thought processes their instructor considered when selecting or creating the problem, including—*What is the key idea in this problem? How is it different from earlier problems? How is it similar?*

## EDUCATIONAL IMPACT

A wide array of quantitative and qualitative methods have been employed to evaluate the educational impact of the SCALE-UP pedagogy. These include classroom observers taking field notes as well as video cameras to record the action. The observer and/or camera can focus on a single group, a table, or how the entire class interacts with the instructor.

The engineering departments were especially interested in knowing if SCALE-UP students could still do typical exam problems, so randomly sampled problems from a mechanics test were selected for student testing. The results are shown in Figure 2. The NCSU SCALE-UP students performed significantly better on all problems except items 10 and 11, which they had not yet covered in class.

**Figure 2**
**Comparison of Traditional and SCALE-UP Students using Randomly Selected Questions from the Traditional Exam.***

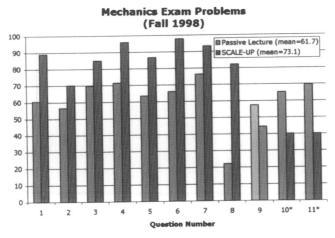

Mechanics Exam Problems
(Fall 1998)

* Item 9 values are not significantly different at the 0.05 level. Items 10 and 11 were not covered in the SCALE-UP class.

The same final exam at the University of Central Florida was given to three lecture sections and a SCALE-UP class, as shown in Figure 3. While not as striking as the mechanics results, in general, the SCALE-UP students outperformed their peers when the material was covered for approximately the same amount of time in both SCALE-UP and traditional classes.

## Figure 3
## Comparing Students with Typical Exam Questions
## (a) Multiple Choice Results
## (b) Problems Requiring Worked Out Solutions*

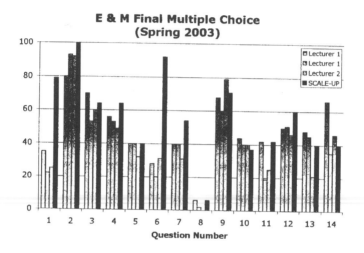

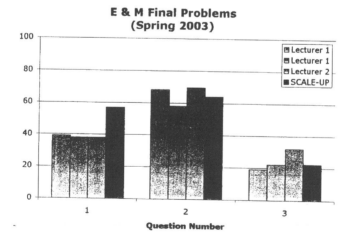

* Item 1 was well covered in SCALE-UP. Item 2 had a
single ponderable. Item 3 had just a demonstration and
ponderable.

**Pass/Fail Rate**

A very coarse, but still useful measure of educational impact is overall pass/fail rate. While not entirely comparable because requirements for traditional and SCALE-UP courses differed, its use was felt to be justified in this analysis since demands were much higher on the SCALE-UP students. (One traditional student mistakenly started taking a SCALE-UP test and asked, *Are we really supposed to know how to do these problems?)*

Figure 4 shows failure rate ratios, calculated by dividing the percentage failing traditional courses by the percentage failing in SCALE-UP. This is over a five-year time span, from 1997 to 2002, and incorporates data from over 16,000 NCSU students. (A student was said to fail the mechanics course when they received a grade lower than C-, since that level of performance barred them from the E & M course. The second semester course was failed with a grade below D-.)

**Figure  4**
**Ratio of Failure Rate Percentages***

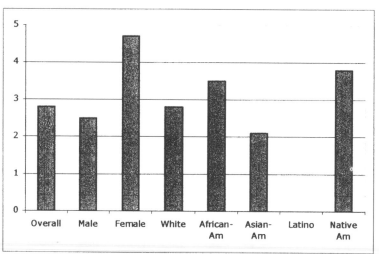

*Overall, students were nearly three times as likely to fail in a traditionally taught section than an equivalent SCALE-UP section of the course. The Latino ratio could not be calculated because no Latino students have failed in a SCALE-UP section.

The results for females and minorities are particularly interesting. Their success has been attributed to the social interactions common in the SCALE-UP environment, where risk-taking is encouraged. If an individual is confused by something, they simply ask their teammate. If their colleague knows the answer, it is explained it to them. If their friend is also confused, they realize they are not alone and will be encouraged to ask the instructor. External evaluators noted the higher quality and quantity of questions in the SCALE-UP classes as compared to the traditional courses.

The investigators also wanted to determine if students were learning concepts, since research has shown that student success and ability to solve traditional problems does not necessarily require real understanding. A variety of research-based tests was employed. Figure 5 shows the FCI (Hestenes, Wells, & Swackhamer, 1992) results for a single instructor (RJB) teaching traditional and SCALE-UP mechanics. Hake's national sample results (Hake, 1998) are shown for comparison. It is clear the SCALE-UP students outperformed their traditionally-taught peers. You can also see when SCALE-UP class size changed from 54 to 99 in the fall of 1999. The benefits of smaller classes cannot be denied.

**Figure 5**

**Normalized Gains on the Force Concept Inventory for Students of a Single Instructor.**

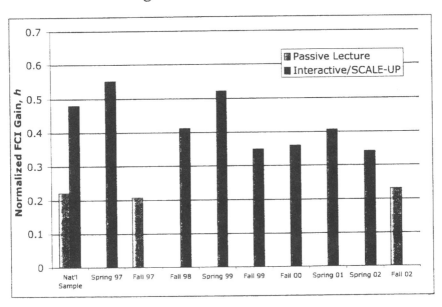

**Low-End Student Concerns**

A common concern of those questioning the need for reform is that a great deal of effort seems to be spent "bringing up the low-end students," perhaps to the detriment of the better students. To see if that was a problem, conceptual test performance for the top, middle, and bottom students in the SCALE-UP classes was examined. What was found is shown in Figure 6.

**Figure 6**
**Results of SCALE-UP Experience by Class Ranking**

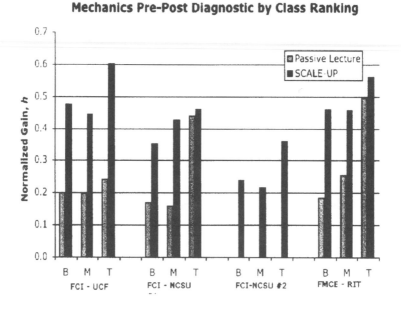

**E & M Pre-Post Diagnostics by Class Ranking**

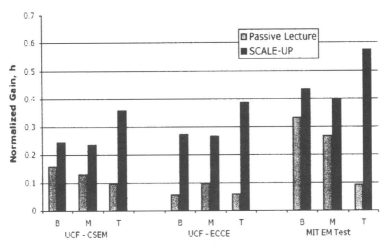

The repeated patterns clearly show that it is the students in the top third of the class who benefit the most from the SCALE-UP pedagogy. The investigators believe this is because these students are probably the ones doing most of the peer-teaching within their group.

What is particularly noteworthy are the data for the top MIT students, arguably the best students in the world. Evidently they have already gathered all they will learn from traditionally taught physics, as evidenced by the very small gain for that cohort. On the other hand, placing top MIT students in the SCALE-UP environment resulted in a huge n, so there was obviously more to be learned.

### Student Attitudes

The investigators felt it was important to assess students' attitudes about the class, but this is a difficult task. A rough measure is to compare attendance rates for students of the same teacher (RJB) when teaching both traditionally and in a SCALE-UP mode. The attendance requirements were identical: students could attend if desired, but there were no direct grade penalties for low attendance.

Table 1 shows that not only was attendance better in SCALE-UP classes, but the spread of attendance rates was lower. The traditional sections always had a few people who rarely attended, driving up the standard deviation values. This was not the case in SCALE-UP.

**Table 1**
**Attendance Rates for Students of the Same Instructor Using Two Modes of Instruction, SCALE-UP and Traditional**

|  | Lecture/Lab | SCALE-UP |
|---|---|---|
| # Classes | 3 | 6 |
| # Students | 263 | 342 |
| % Attendance | 75.2 | 90.3 |
| Std. Dev. | 24.0 | 11.6 |

Quotes from interviews also provide insight into how students viewed the SCALE-UP classes. It is interesting to compare the impressions students have of their colleagues in the following two quotes:

> *I can deal with the lecture class, it's just that I enjoy more...getting more into the interactive projects. It's more hands on. If you don't understand something, you just ask the guy next to you. Nobody yells at you for talking*

*...you have a professor right in the middle and...a couple of guys spread out and you can flag them down...In the lecture, you are sitting...25 rows back. You really don't have anyone but the two people next to you and they don't know. You really don't have anyone with some knowledge to help you out*

## Performance in Later Classes

The real test of an educational reform is student performance in later classes. SCALE-UP Mechanics students were found to do significantly better in their E & M course (whether the later course is taught traditionally or in the SCALE-UP mode). Their performance was found to be slightly, but  significantly worse than that of traditional students in Engineering Statics courses. This caused concern until it was realized that a substantially larger fraction of students were passing SCALE-UP sections. Those students would have never been admitted to the engineering course if they had taken a traditional physics course and failed.

To see if this might be the case SAT scores were used as a way of identifying students at risk of failure in traditional physics. As expected, there was no difference in passing rates for those students with Math SAT scores above 500. But of those students whose Math SAT was less than 500, 83% of the SCALE-UP students passed Engineering Statics compared to only 69% of the traditionally-taught students. So physics is no longer the "filter" it used to be. What's more, students who probably would not have progressed toward an engineering degree with traditional physics instruction are succeeding in their later courses.

## DISSEMINATION

A large number of schools have adopted the SCALE-UP approach and have adapted it to their particular circumstances. Figure 7 shows a few of their classrooms.

**Figure 7**
**SCALE-UP Classrooms at American University, University of Central Florida, MIT, and University of New Hampshire.***

*Note the modified table design in the last photo

The investigators are encouraging other institutions to adopt the SCALE-UP approach by providing classroom design assistance, presenting talks and workshops, and by producing a Website (Beichner, 2003) with lesson plans and teacher guides. This has been quite successful and the number of schools using this approach is increasing. Assistance is available to any who are considering adopting this approach by sending an e-mail to saul@physics.ucf.edu or beichner@ncsu.edu or by visiting the Website.

Some of what has been learned from the SCALE-UP project has also resulted in changes in a "mainstream" physics text (Serway & Beichner, 2000). Tangible activities are called *QuickLabs* while ponderable activities are labeled *Quick Quizzes*. More than 1/3 of all science, math, and engineering majors in the U.S. are using materials developed as part of the SCALE-UP project. Figure 8 shows samples of these from the book.

**Figure 8**
*SCALE-UP Materials in Serway & Beichner's "Physics for Scientists and*

QuickLab

Determine the thickness of a page
from this book. (Note that numbers
that have no measurement errors—
like the count of a number of
pages—do not affect the significant
figures in a calculation.) In terms of
significant figures, why is it better to
measure the thickness of as many
pages as possible and then divide by
the number of sheets?

*Engineers"*

Quick Quiz 36.5

Which glasses in Figure 36.38 correct nearsightedness and which correct farsightedness?

(a)                    (b)

# REFERENCES

Arons, A (1990). *A guide to introductory physics teaching.*
New York: Wiley.

Astin, A. W. (1993). What matters in college? *Four critical
years revisited* (1st ed.). San Francisco: Jossey-Bass.

Beichner, R. *SCALE-UP Physics Webpage.* Retrieved July,
2003 from http://scaleup.ncsu.edu.

Beichner, R., Bernold, L., Burniston, E., Dali, P., Felder, R., Gastineau, M., & Risley, J. (1999). Case study of the physics component of an integrated curriculum. Physics Education Research Supplement to *American Journal of Physics, 67*( 7), S16.

Christian, W., & Belloni, M. (2001). *Physlets: Teaching physics with interactive curricular material* (1st ed.) Upper Saddle River, NJ: Prentice-Hall.

Coleman, L. A., Holcomb, D. F., & Rigden, J. S. (1998). The introductory university physics project 1987-1995: What has it accomplished? *American Journal of Physics,* 66(2), 124.

Fagan, A. P., Crouch, C. H., & Mazur, E. (2002). Peer instruction: Results from a range of classrooms. *Physics Teacher, 40,* 206.

Hake, R. R. (1992). Socratic pedagogy in the introductory physics laboratory. *Physics Teacher, 30,* 546.

Hake, R. R.(1998). Interactive-engagement vs. traditional methods: A six-thousand-student survey of mechanics test data for introductory physics courses. *American Journal of Physics, 66*(1), 64.

Heller, P. M., Keith, R., & Anderson, S. (1992). Teaching problem solving through cooperative grouping. Part 1: Group versus individual problem solving. *American Journal of Physics, 60,* 627.

Hestenes, D., Wells, M., & Swackhamer, G. (1992). Force concept inventory. *Physics Teacher,* 30(3), 141.

Johnson, D. W., Johnson, R. T., & Smith, K. A. (1991). *Cooperative learning: Increasing college faculty instructional productivity.* Washington, D.C.: George Washington University, School of Education and Human Development.

Knight, R. (2000). *Studio classes at CalPoly: What have we learned?* Retrieved January, 2005 from http://chemweb. calpoly.edu/phys.

Laws, P. W. (1991). Calculus-based physics without lectures. *Physics Today, 44*(8), 24.

Laws, P. W. (1997). Millikan lecture 1996: Promoting active learning based on physics education research in introductory physics courses. *American Journal of Physics, 65*(1), 13.

Mazur, E. (1997). *Peer instruction.* Upper Saddle River, NJ: Prentice-Hall.

McDermott, L. C. (1991). Millikan lecture 1990: What we teach and what is learned—closing the gap. *American Journal of Physics, 59,* 301.

McDermott, L. C., & Redish, E. F. (1999). Resource letter: PER-1: Physics Education Research. *American Journal of Physics, 67*(9), 755.

McDermott, L. C., Shaffer, P. S., & the Physics Education Group. (1998). *Tutorials in introductory physics.* Upper Saddle River, NJ: Prentice-Hall.

Polya, G. (1973). *How to solve it: A new aspect of mathematical method* (2nd ed.). Princeton, NJ: Princeton University Press.

Redish, E. F., Saul, J. M., & Steinberg, R. N. (1997). On the effectiveness of active-engagement microcomputer-based laboratories. *American Journal of Physics, 65*(1), 45.

Redish, E. F., & Steinberg, R. N. (1999). Teaching physics: Figuring out what works. *Physics Today, 52* (January), 24.

Saul, J. M. (1998). *Beyond problem-solving: Evaluating introductory physics courses through the hidden curriculum.* Unpublished dissertation, University of Maryland.

Serway, R. A., & Beichner, R. J. (2000). *Physics for scientists and engineers, with modern physics* (5th ed.). Fort Worth: Saunders College Publishing.

Sokoloff, D. R., & Thornton, R. K. (1997). Using interactive lecture demonstrations to create an active learning environment. *Physics Teacher, 35*, 340.

Van Heuvelen, A. (1991). Learning to think like a physicist: A review of research-based instructional strategies. *American Journal of Physics, 59*, 891.

Wilson, J. M. (1994). The CUPLE physics studio. *Physics Teacher, 32*, 518.

**Note.** The authors would like to thank the FIPSE program of the U.S. Department of Education (PB116B71905 & P116B000659), the National Science Foundation (DUE-9752313 & DUE-9981107), Hewlett Packard, Apple Computer, and Pasco Scientific for their support. They would also like to thank the members of the physics education research groups at North Carolina State University and the University of Central Florida, and collaborators working at Coastal Carolina University, the University of New Hampshire, MIT and the Rochester Institute of Technology, for their contributions to the paper.

# INDIVIDUALISM, COMMUNITY

# AND ACADEMIC INTEGRITY

## Nancy A. Stanlick
### University Of Central Florida

## INTRODUCTION

In principle, students attend colleges and universities to receive an education and prepare for a profession. To cheat or plagiarize in pursuit of that goal, however, is to deprive oneself of an education and to call seriously into question one's proficiency for successful practice in her field. There are many reasons that students cheat, but first and foremost, the cheater is looking for a good (or at least a passing) grade. The underlying reason is, in fact, the desire to pass. And this is much of the essence of the problem of academic dishonesty—the cheater is trying to pass herself or himself off as something s/he is not.

Solving, or at least reducing the problem of academic dishonesty, may be best determined by trying to find a root cause that goes much farther to the heart of the matter than the simple pursuit of a good grade. Pursuing a good grade alone, and cheating to get it, is likely a symptom of a more serious underlying problem. The underlying problem may be this society's general conception of the goal(s) of education and its orientation toward individualism that creates an atmosphere in which cheating is the rule rather than the exception. If that conception of the goal of education could be changed and the benefits of education seen instead as relevant to the

171

interests of an entire community, a beginning might be made in reducing instances of academic dishonesty.

## LIBERAL INDIVIDUALISM, COMPETITION, AND ACADEMIC DISHONESTY

Bernard Gert (2000) contends that to solve the problem of academic dishonesty, we should understand education as competitive. Conceiving of education in this way, one assumes both that education is competitive and that students see it that way. As a competitive enterprise, according to Gert, students who cheat disadvantage (cheat) honest others. As competition, the goal of education is to do the best that one can and do better than others. The cheater, however, only appears to be better than others, thus depriving the honest student of appropriately deserved respect and benefits attending actual success.

To conceive of the goals and purpose of education on a competitive, liberal individualistic model such as that put forward by Bernard Gert (2000) is, I think, to understand education and our social relations such that we are essentially competitors for scarce resources in a world populated by self-interested utility maximizers who cooperate (do not cheat) with others only when it serves their own interests. When it does not do so, or when it appears necessary to by-pass cooperation and integrity to achieve an individual goal, self-interest will take hold and lead to uncooperative (cheating) behaviors. Perhaps part of the reason that academic dishonesty is such a serious problem is that many educators and students conceive of education and their role in it on the liberal individualistic model.

An analysis of Gert's (2000) position on the problem of cheating may show the paucity of the competitive, individualistic model of education. Doing the best that one can seems innocuous enough. To do the best that one can is consistent with doing so not only for oneself, but also for a more overriding or common good. To claim, however, that a goal of education is to do better than others smacks of individualism gone awry because it encourages cheating for the purported benefit to the individual in passing oneself off as successful when one is not.

To support the claim that the goal of education is to do better than others, Gert (2000) contends that if academic activity is concerned only with learning and improving academic skills, other people involved in the same activity would not care when someone cheats. But since others do care when someone cheats, it follows that academic activities are not concerned only with learning and improving academic skills. Gert concludes that education is competitive.

But the conclusion that education is competitive does not follow from the premises. All that follows from the notion that people care when someone cheats is that activities are not concerned only with learning and improving academic skills for the individual alone.  Gert (2000) does not deny that part of the purpose of education is to learn and improve academic skills.  He denies, however, that it is the only purpose. In this respect, it is not difficult to agree with him. But it is not necessary to agree that academic activities are or should be competitive, or that the reason others complain when someone cheats is that the cheater has cheated only the honest student.

Gert's (2000) position is that when students understand that education is competitive, they will become actively involved in prevention of academic dishonesty and will not tolerate it. He proposes that students take a vote at the beginning of each semester whether they prefer to have examinations proctored. His view is that no matter how they vote, it shows that students do not approve of cheating. So if they choose to have examinations proctored, they are concerned about the problem of academic dishonesty. And if they choose not to have examinations proctored, it shows that they think that cheating is not a problem. Further, however, if there are students who vote for no proctoring and cheat, anyway, they are beyond the point where something can be done for them (Gert, 2000).

What is wrong with Gert's (2000) argument depends on the assumption that education is competitive and that students believe that those who cheat, cheat only the non-cheaters. Those assumptions are clearly mistaken—especially since students often help others to cheat. Yet Gert explains that if education is not competitive, then prohibitions against cheating are only paternalistic rules that have no moral force. He supports this contention by claiming that if education is only about knowledge and improving one's own academic skills, no one will care when the cheater cheats. But other people do care, and he claims that this leads to the conclusion that education is a competitive activity, and that it is about doing better than others. This author believes, however, that it does not follow from Gert's premises that if education is not competitive that prohibitions against cheating are only paternalistic rules having no moral implications.

Prohibitions against cheating that come from within the individual as a member of a community of others engaged in the same sort of activity are not paternalistic rules. They are, instead, highly moral and have important moral implications for the society in which we live, and for the individual himself. Since Gert's (2000) position revolves around the notion that cheaters cheat only other students, his position does not take adequate account of the interconnectedness of individuals and communities of which they are members, and the way in which the success or proficiency of members of a group has implications far beyond the bounds of mere competition.

The inadequacy of the liberal individualistic, competitive view of education is shown in Gert's (2000) conceptualization of cheating in academics as analogous to a game. Gert explains that in golf (or any other sport), one does not say that a cheater cheated the referees or the game itself. The cheater has cheated other players. But understanding education as a competitive game lacks attention to the role and place of all members of the academic community and the moral implications of academic dishonesty for that community.

The claim that cheaters cheat other students is not objectionable. However, there is much more to it than this. The cheater also cheats herself or himself, faculty members, and the academic and social communities to which s/he belongs. Gert (2000) seems, in fact, to agree that this is the case when he claims that the cheater is arrogant, and that the real danger is that this arrogance is likely to show itself in realms other than the academic. It is clear that the cheater is arrogant, believing that rules and standards do not apply to her or him, but the arrogance of the cheater implies something about the effects of cheating on the larger society of which education is a part.

Gert (2000), using the analogy to a game, conceives only of limited relationships between individuals in a community (students), and not the relationships that students have to all others who are part of a community. For example, Gert claims that faculty members are like referees whose job it is to protect honest students from cheaters in the same way that the job of a referee in basketball is to detect and penalize players for inappropriate plays and behavior.

Understanding the problem of cheating and the role of faculty members in preventing it as Gert (2000) does rests on the notion that cheating depends on a social institution rather than social interaction. This, however, is another indication of the narrow focus of Gert's position in that he fails to recognize that an academic community consists of many others, not simply students. He claims that cheating "is not obeying the rules of an activity when everyone participating in that activity is expected and required to do so" (1998, p. 192). According to Gert, then, cheating is different from breaking a promise or deceiving someone because there are activities in which a person may participate in which there is no one to whom an explicit or implicit promise was made.

Even, however, if there is no explicit promise made between "players" in a game, that does not imply that there are no responsibilities of individuals toward others or toward the community that makes playing the game possible. Gert's (2000) failure to recognize this fact leads to an explicit contradiction. If he is right that education is competitive, it then makes no sense to say that one can compete with others without social interaction, and it is certainly not the case that a competitor is competing with a social institution. One competes, then, in a social context. It follows, then, that Gert's claim that cheating depends on a social institution rather than social interaction is simply false because social interaction in education occurs between all members of the academic community. So Gert's proposal that faculty members serve as referees in a competitive educational game and that cheating is not part of social interaction is narrow and short-sighted.

If the author is correct that education is not and should not be competitive, that cheating is not only cheating other students, and that education is an activity in which people engage as a part of a community for the benefit of that community, then faculty members are not referees, they are players in Gert's (2000) educational "game" and are harmed when cheaters cheat.

In fact, in continuing with Gert's (2000) educational game analogy, we see that players in a game are not coached or taught by referees. Those who teach or coach players in a sport are interested and involved in players' and teams' success. Students and faculty are all on the same team, so to speak, and pursuing the same goal. It is to win for the team as well as for the team's individual members.

If the above is the case, competition in a game is a social activity, depending on interaction with others. And since coaches and players, like faculty and students, are on the "same team," and coaches are interested and have a stake in the success of the team and its individual players, an honest coach will not see her or his role simply as policing players to ensure that they do not cheat. An honest coach encourages team work, recognizing that the group works together to achieve a common goal, and that the actual talent or proficiency of players enhances the team.

The rugged individualist player who does not follow the rules affects everyone from spectators to consumers to other players to the coach. The actions of the cheater affect others in that they devalue the team on the whole. Because the expertise of individual players affects the success of the team, it is essential that players are, in fact, all better players in the game and do not simply appear to be so, or just pass as being good players when they are not. The idea is not to pass as a successful person in sport or academics. The idea and the ideal is to pass as in fact being successful in sport or academics (the community) of which one is a part.

## AN ALTERNATIVE, COMMUNITY-BASED APPROACH TO ACADEMIC INTEGRITY

It is contrary to the spirit of the academic community, to the prevention of academic dishonesty, and to the goals of education to conceive of education as a competitive activity similar to a game. The goals of education are not, as Gert (2000) would have it, to do the best that one can and do better than others. The goals are to do and be the best that one can and to do better for oneself and others. Education, then, should not be understood or promoted as a competitive enterprise. It is, instead, and should be, cooperative and community-dependent, and this conception of education is at least the beginning of the creation of an effective means to combat and prevent academic dishonesty.

Students who violate an academic code of conduct are not recalcitrant players in a competitive game, but are violators of the spirit of the academic community of which they are a part, and who cheat every member of that community. To focus on community rather than the single-minded pursuit of individual success is to cultivate an environment of respect for education, for the community, and for its members. It is to recognize and foster a conception of cheating and academic dishonesty that combats academic dishonesty when the members of an academic community have respect for themselves and for that community and see the attainment of educational goals as much more than the individual pursuit of personal success.

Noah and Eckstein (2001) explain that fraud (cheating, plagiarism) is such an important topic because it has implications for the larger social group. They note that:

> ...exam results and credentials serve as evidence, even guarantees, of competence. Those who complete training and studies in a given field are assumed to be competent to enter a society's workforce and perform their responsibilities at given levels of effectiveness...If they are false, all aspects of the functioning of society suffer" (p. 21).

The point is that the academic community fails when the individual fails to achieve real proficiency and competence, when the individual passes as proficient and competent, but in fact is not. And because the educational community is part of an even larger society, the implications of passing are serious indeed.

To pass is one thing. To be competent is another. It is necessary to conceptualize and put into practice the meaning of academic integrity that is consistent with the role of the individual as part of a community of cooperating individuals striving toward common goals. Achieving a sense of community is realized through recognizing and acting on our obligations to ourselves and others. To do this, one should revisit the competitive model of education to be able to reject it and see that even though it may mirror this society, it would be better to attempt to change the image and alter the reflection.

Kibler, Nuss, Paterson & Pavela (1998) refer to the distinction between social periods of individual ascendancy and periods of community ascendancy and point out that "our current social, political and economic circumstances are indicative of a period of individual ascendancy" (p. 4) in that it is a "time in which incidents of dishonesty may be more prevalent" (p 4) than at other times (in periods of community ascendancy). "Community ascendancy is characterized by future orientation, asceticism, concern for responsibility, and a duty to others. In contrast, individual ascendancy is characterized by a present orientation, hedonism, a concern for rights, and a duty to self" (p, 4).

Perhaps Gert's (2000) understanding of education is informed by this rights-based, self-interested, individual ascendancy orientation of the society in which we live. It is a system in which there are rules of conduct that get in the way of people's "success" and that are sidestepped when the opportunity to do so presents itself. If an individual is concerned primarily or solely with his own interests, the interests and concerns of the community may be set aside.

Gert (2000) claims that this competitive, individualistic approach will help to solve the problem of academic dishonesty because non-cheaters will police the cheaters, forcing them to abide by the rules and expelling them from the community of individuals when they are caught. Unfortunately, it is unlikely that this approach to the problem will do more than stave off the problem briefly, and only until competitors figure out how to break the rules without getting caught.

Academic dishonesty could be prevented more effectively and reliably when people see themselves as part of a community, and in which they have responsibilities to it such that passing is not more important than real success and honesty. McCabe, Trevino and Butterfield (1999), for example, have found that:

> Most (honor) code students see themselves as part of a moral community that offers significant trust and freedom and has corresponding rules and expectations that must be honored to preserve that trust and freedom. Previous quantitative research on cheating ..., and the comments offered by students in this analysis, suggest that this community approach is quite effective in controlling academic dishonesty among college students (p 226).

If students are likely to be dishonest less often when they are aware of and acknowledge an honor code, perhaps it is because that code is something they have embraced for themselves and for their community, and have done so willingly with their acceptance as members of a community from which they will receive valuable benefits and real self-improvement and to which they are expected to contribute for the good of others. For students who see themselves simply as present in a community, but not as a part of it, passing oneself off as competent may be sufficient because the community is not of central concern on the competitive model. But for the student who respects the community and recognizes the interrelated interdependency of the self and others, the creation of a sense of community builds:

> "…an institutional culture in which cheating and plagiarism are condemned as something that 'our people' just don't do. In this way…rules and regulations, enforcement and penalties, become minor aspects of the academic scene. All members of the campus community will have integrated in their own attitudes and behavior a set of expectations and values that makes the regulatory and punitive approach not only unnecessary but even counterproductive" (Noah and Eckstein, 2001, p. 140).

Paradoxically, perhaps, creating such communities is also good for the person bent on individual ascendancy—s/he cannot ascend in a community of honesty and integrity without accepting and acting on its values.

## CONCLUSIONS

To hold and act consistently with a liberal individualistic, competitive and self-interested model of education is not a means to combat the problem of academic dishonesty. It is detrimental to the creation of academic communities that foster a sense of belonging and a conception of responsibility to others as well as to oneself.

To cheat is to violate an academic community and to ignore one's responsibilities. This is not to say that cheaters do not cheat other students. But to see cheating simply as a matter of cheating only other students  provides the cheater with motivation only not to cheat based on the fear of censure or punishment meted out by the community. It does nothing to change the motivation to cheat.

Building an academic (or any other) community requires honesty, integrity, and a commitment to that community's values. The individualistic, competitive view lacks, then, appropriate incentive not to cheat. If education is competitive, it does not follow that the reason not to cheat is that others will not allow the cheater the opportunity to gain the benefits of the activity if s/he does cheat, as Gert (2000) contends. The cheater will, instead, try to find more and better ways to cheat and not be caught doing so. Thinking of education as competitive, then, does not solve the problem of academic dishonesty because it does nothing to remove the incentive to cheat.

A more effective way to combat and prevent the problem of cheating may be to build educational and other communities in which all members of the community interact with each other as members who have something to contribute to it, whose contributions are valued, and who feel a sense of obligation to each other and to the values that inform it. Everyone in an educational community has an interest in others passing. But no one's interests are served by any individual simply passing as something that one is not.

## REFERENCES

Gert, B. (1998). *Morality: Its nature and justification.* New York: Oxford University Press.

Gert, B. (2000). *Academic integrity.* Retrieved January 1, 2005 from http://ethics.sandiego.edu/Resources/cai/webworkshop/Gert/Cheating.html.

Kibler, W. L., Nuss, E. M., Paterson, B. G., &. Pavela, G. (1998). *Academic integrity and student development: Legal issues, policy perspectives.* Ashville, NC: College Administration Publications.

McCabe, D. L., Trevino, L. K., & Butterfield. K. D. (1999). Academic integrity in honor code and non-honor code environments: A qualitative investigation. *Journal of Higher Education, 70*(2), 211-34.

Noah, H. J, & Eckstein, M. A. (2001). *Fraud and education: The worm in the apple.* Lanham, MD.: Rowman & Littlefield.

# INTEGRATING LEARNING,

# REFLECTIVE E-PORTFOLIOS,

# UNDERGRADUATE RESEARCH

# AND ASSESSMENT

**Benjamin R. Stephens**
**Barbara E. Weaver**
*Clemson University*

## INTRODUCTION

Strategies and techniques for promoting and evaluating integrative learning at the programmatic level are explored in this paper. The core of the approach lies in the use of technology to facilitate adaptation of reflective e-portfolios.

Before examining the elements of this approach, it may be helpful to understand the nature of the undergraduate psychology curriculum at Clemson University where this study was conducted—and how technology, particularly laptop-facilitated laboratories, eased the transformation to the current undergraduate program. As in most psychology curricula, majors complete a required core of specific courses in addition to courses selected from a menu of domains within this and allied disciplines. There is no capstone experience, though many students enroll in faculty-mentored research and thesis courses.

For a research-oriented department this curriculum seemed typical and effective. *So what were the problems that technology helped to solve?* One problem was the relatively weak assessment. There were few bases for the detection of lower achievement—this needed improvement. Second, there was no technique to guide, document, or assess students' integration of learning goals and outcomes within the discipline nor across psychology and allied disciplines.

Technology facilitated the adaptation of solutions to theses limitations through laptop pedagogy, particularly reflective e-portfolios, writing labs, and research labs (Stephens, in press). Today, the department has a new introductory lab, laptop pedagogy supporting the statistics and methods courses, and a new senior capstone lab. The new Introductory and Senior labs are required only for majors, are one-credit-hour courses, and so were relatively low-cost additions to the curriculum. The assessment strategy is embedded in these laboratories, and sets the stage for understanding students' educational achievements as well as enhancing their abilities to integrate their understandings across the broader academic experience.

## WHY REFLECTIVE E-PORTFOLIOS?

A reflective e-portfolio seems to be a powerful technique for effective integrative learning. Many argue persuasively that reflection may be crucial for integrative learning (American Psychological Association, 2003; Huber and Hutchings, 2004; Yancey, 2001). Yancey (1998) argues that reflection lets students assume responsibility for documenting and interpreting their own learning, and that this exercise forces students to give visibility to their thinking and consequently promotes constructive learning and deeper understanding. These processes are consistent with prevailing cognitive theory and principles, such as an apprenticeship model of cognitive development and assessment (Gardner, 1992), as well as socially mediated cognition that is domain specific (Brown et al, 1992; Vygotsky, 1978). These cognitive viewpoints suggest that mentored examination of self-defined achievement, as in reflective e-portfolios, is fertile ground for development of deeper critical thinking skills.

## Scope of E-Portfolios

The scope of reflective e-portfolio can vary. Class e-portfolios ask students to indicate their understanding of course material over the course of the term. A program e-portfolio, located within a discipline, requires students to reflect on and provide evidence of their competence across the discipline. For example, engineering departments recently have embraced reflective program e-portfolios in response to the accreditation demands of their discipline (Panitz, 1988). Many engineering departments see the e-portfolio as a rich data source that can document student achievement of goals prescribed by ABET-2000 accreditation criteria, or state legislation (Berg & Nasr, 2002; Olds & Pavelich, 1996; Pigott & Karr, 2001).

The program e-portfolio may also be used by students to acquire jobs, and so students readily appreciate its value. The psychology department student e-portfolios include a resume, and so may prompt student-defined integrating themes between the college curriculum, extracurricular activities, personal development, and career development (Garcia & Clausen, 2000; Kwiatkowski, 2003; Yancey & Weiser, 1997).

## Relation to Undergraduate Research

In addition to these functions, electronic e-portfolios may well share pedagogical elements common to "best practices" for undergraduate science education. This attribute enhances the value of the e-portfolio for science education, engages student attention, and should reinforce common elements of critical thinking skills.

Undergraduate research experiences effectively promote understanding and interest in science via active involvement of the student in an original inquiry (Boyer Commission, 1998; National Science Foundation, 1996), leading to critical thinking in a mentored context suitable for effective pedagogical strategies (Kardash, 2000). The activities, goals, and processes involved in e-portfolio construction seem quite similar to those of undergraduate research. The e-portfolio activities and goals also are active, authentic, goal-oriented, and may produce a product of value to the student.

The processes of collection, selection, and reflection are similar to the processes of scientific research. As with data collection, e-portfolio students collect potential evidence. Selection in e-portfolios is conceptually similar to hypothesis formation and evaluation; in both, data are organized and assessed conceptually and logically. Theoretical synthesis and evaluation seem similar to the process of reflection; in both, a student weighs and integrates the collected evidence to construct new understandings. Thus, the reflective e-portfolio may be effective as a learning experience and as an assessment base for the scientific curriculum.

## INTEGRATING LEARNING VIA E-PORTFOLIOS

Integrative learning as used here refers to student constructed connections within and across domain-specific knowledge systems (Huber & Hutchings, 2004; Shavelson & Huang, 2003). Experience using the approach described here may elucidate the meanings, techniques, and types of evidence for integrative learning. This understanding is central for transfer of the lessons learned within and across disciplines. The authors are developing methods to describe these connections through multiple measures, obtained across the semester and class rank. Such measurement can reveal developmental differences which point to potential factors that promote integrative learning.

Students make connections for themselves to support a range of e-portfolio goals. In the Intro lab, a common goal is developmental, where students' lab e-portfolios communicate a deepening appreciation of fundamental concepts across psychology and beyond. The Methods e-portfolio is a "course e-portfolio," designed to communicate mastery of the course objectives. A common goal in the Senior lab is a "show-case" program e-portfolio, communicating both psychology and non-psychology themes to graduate schools or employers. Thus, integrative learning is intentional. Importantly, the students' learning is about self. Their understandings, their interests and their capabilities are integrated across domains, and as such represent a metacognitve skill containing the reflective process of self-examined understandings of self.

E-portfolio construction (collection, selection, and reflection) promotes this metacognitive skill. The construction is a direct, active, and communicated model for cyclical and synergistic discovery. Across the semester, the repeated sequence of collection, selection, and reflection provides the student with multiple samples sharing the same process structure. Such multiple experiences provide the mental model for student understanding of integration as a general process involved in creative, critical, and scientific endeavors.

**Curricular Enhancements in the Psychology Program**

All courses outlined below were designed and structured to guide student integrative learning through the reflective e-portfolio construction process. Students communicate curricular and extracurricular experiences through this framework. A Web-based support system was employed to guide the collection, selection, and reflection cycles of student's activities and e-portfolio construction (see http://people.clemson.edu/~bstephe).

*Intro Lab Structure.* In the Intro Lab, laptop pedagogy facilitated the integrative goal, guiding the students' ability to construct and communicate their understanding of connecting themes, mainly within psychology, but also across disciplines. Writing laboratories are employed in the collection, selection, and reflection phases.

In the collection phase, collections of descriptions and notes are solicited from the student in a series of open-ended questions designed for the specific experiment or demonstration. The process of selection from these collected experiences is guided by the faculty. Such selections are the organized experiences which students believe promote their learning and understanding of the phenomena and concepts.

In the reflection phase, students are prompted to formulate connections between the selected concepts and other lab experiences, lecture experiences, non-psychology course experiences, extracurricular activities, career goals, and personal development. Students also construct a fantasy resume, connections to degree requirements, and educational goals. The product is a Web-based e-portfolio, which is periodically reviewed and enhanced with student-defined integrating themes

*Methods Course Structure.* For the Methods course, students' understanding of the elements of scientific research is developed through a series of group experiments culminating in a capstone project independently developed by each student. Technology-facilitated improvements in the "Research Methods" course resulted in easing the students' ability to integrate these experiences via the course e-portfolio (Stephens, in press).

Laptops facilitate class digital e-portfolios construction. Materials are easily organized and constructed in brief in-class updating and revision sessions throughout the semester, culminating in a final revision process that includes peer review and revision during the last week of the semester.

Experimental research projects (data collection, analysis, report writing) are integrated across laboratory and class meetings. Students design, execute and evaluate their research experiments using their laptops as course demands and needs dictate. They prepare reports via flexible 10-35 minute laptop writing laboratories.

Student understanding and engagement appears to improve through these "on-demand" organizational and e-portfolio activities. There also is a marked increase in instructor-student interaction as the lines between "class-time" and "lab-time" became productively blurred as the semester progressed.

Many students' e-portfolios offer reflective pieces that highlight improved understandings that accompany higher quality written reports. Most students seem to sense the synergistic interplay between understanding and communication. The portfolios show evidence of students' ability to think critically; they convey a sense of the students' excitement and competence.

***Senior Lab Structure.*** For the Senior Lab, faculty guide integrative learning across psychology and general domains through construction of the resume and psychology program e-portfolio using the same elements of collection, selection, and reflection. In e-portfolio construction, a collection phase (e.g. list all courses, collect all papers and artifacts) and a selection phase (identify and justify the artifacts that were central to understanding, capability, career development, etc.) are employed.

In the reflection phase, students organize and identify integrating constructs to characterize their educational experiences. Construction of resume and graduate school applications also employ the same collection, selection and reflection processes. For example, the resume links to work samples and artifacts associated with psychology course work, non-psychology course work, and extracurricular activities (e.g. internships, summer research experiences, etc.). The communication of these major integrating themes is supported with the selected artifacts and communicated in a professional, student-centered, Web-based e-portfolio.

**Assessment Embedded in Course Activities and E-Portfolios**.

To gauge integrative learning, qualitative evidence in the classroom in the form of student engagement, apparent understanding, etc. is sought. Finding positive signs, the next step is to look for quantitative measures such as increased intercorrelations and increased scores (across semester and for each rank) within and across measures of domain-specific knowledge.

*The Psychological Assessment Survey*. Domain-specific knowledge is measured through the use of a self-report and an e-portfolio version of the Psychology Assessment Survey (Stephens & Moore, 2004). The Psychology Assessment Survey contains 169 target goals and outcomes from five domains of achievement in psychology (i.e. Knowledge Base, Research Methods, Critical Thinking Skills, Application, and Values) and five domains of general achievement (i.e. Information and Technological Literacy, Communication Skills, Sociocultural and International Awareness, Personal Development, and Career Planning Development) derived from national learning goals and outcomes (American Psychological Association, 2003). Four items specifying phantom target abilities were included to tap Response Bias.

Early data suggest acceptable reliability and validity of the self-report version of the instrument (Stephens & Moore, 2004). More recently, confirmatory factor analysis, based on a sample of 1157 undergraduates, demonstrates that the American Psychological Association (2003) hierarchical structure is consistent with student Psychology Assessment Survey ratings, but only when Response Bias is controlled. This result increases the sense of acceptable validity, since the removal of effects due to response bias implies that the remaining pattern of results may not be biased.

Each student completes a non-portfolio Psychology Assessment Survey at the beginning of the semester. At the end of the semester, each student completes a non-portfolio Psychology Assessment Survey and an e-portfolio-based Psychology Assessment Survey. Peer and instructor e-portfolio-based Psychology Assessment Survey measures also are collected. (E-portfolio-based Psychology Assessment Survey scores are derived from review and analysis of the e-portfolio and are used to further validate concurrent non-portfolio self-report Psychology Assessment Survey measures.)

***Anticipated Results.*** With data collection to be completed at semester's end, it's expected that mean Psychology Assessment Survey scale scores (and intercorrelations among scales) in psychology and general domains should increase in strength over the semester if students' e-portfolio construction promotes integrative learning. These increased intercorrelations and scale scores in psychology and general domains should be stronger in the Senior lab (compared to the Intro lab) if greater experience enhances the benefits of integrative teaching.

Importantly, the authors anticipate acceptable convergence among non-portfolio-based self-ratings and portfolio-based self ratings, peer ratings, and instructor ratings. Such convergence could reduce the primary practical barrier to e-portfolio-based assessment, namely the labor intensive process of independent external scoring of the e-portfolios. Since the convergence described here is among raters and activities embedded within the courses' normal semester structure, the assessment strategy does not routinely entail additional external labor.

***Preliminary Observations.*** Early observations promote optimism—students' e-portfolio artifacts can provide a rich and effective source for assessment. For example, recall that the Introductory course students conduct several demonstration experiments leading to brief written reports, and they include these reports in their e-portfolio. To determine if these reports are effective in assessment, a pilot lab study was conducted with non-majors from an honors section of Introductory Psychology (Stephens, in press). The 23 students met in a desktop computer lab, simulating a laptop class. A Web-based module demonstrated a face discrimination experiment. After the demonstration, each student constructed her/his own hypothesis, collected data through the Web interface, analyzed the results, and completed a written report. Over three consecutive 75-minute meetings, attendance was near 100% despite the fact that the experience was "extra-credit" only.

The reports seemed impressive, gauged against the skills and knowledge of the typical introductory student, despite the fact that the students knew that the reports would not be graded. To guard against rater bias, a senior undergraduate student also read each report, and rated the author's understanding of ten main elements of research compared to a "B-average" Introductory Psychology student, and then compared to a "B-average" Research Methods student.

These independent ratings indicated that the introductory authors were viewed as similar to Research Methods students on four elements and as better than typical Introductory Psychology students on eight elements. This evaluation supported the notion that the module produced an artifact that enabled potentially effective assessment.

## E-PORTFOLIOS
## IN UNDERGRADUATE RESEARCH

A similar reflective e-portfolio technique was employed to enhance intern learning goals and outcomes in a National Science Foundation Research Experience for Undergraduates Summer Program in Applied Psychology at Clemson University. The Summer Program in Applied Psychology provides student participants with research training in human factors, industrial/organizational, and health psychology.

### Summer Program in Applied Psychology

The objectives of the Summer Program in Applied Psychology at Clemson University are to increase talented students' interest, understanding, and commitment to research, science, and scientific careers. These objectives are anticipated to increase and sustain student participation in research, professional activities, and entry into graduate programs.

Students selected for this program have strong backgrounds in mathematics, biological science, social science, and/or industrial engineering, exhibit potential interest and commitment to science and research, and are selected mainly from non-research colleges and universities. Program activities include a supervised program of collaborative research with 11 participating faculty from the Psychology and Industrial Engineering Departments.

Support activities include course work in research methods in applied psychology, seminars, site-visits and the Conference in Applied Psychology. Research partners in industry, government and education collaborate via participation in support activities and research projects. Students present the results of their research at the Conference on Applied Psychology, which includes presentations from invited speakers. Follow-through annual activities include travel support for additional professional presentations, collaborative publications and advising to support applications to graduate programs.

**Achieving Program Objectives**

Program objectives are achieved through mentored authentic research projects in the context of multiple support systems. A central support system was the summer program e-portfolio. This program e-portfolio was designed to document activities that might enhance education in the program's intellectual focus, development and completion of student research projects and student career development. The artifacts included materials from class activities, research presentations and manuscripts as well as reflections on these artifacts. These products were organized in each participant's e-portfolio throughout the summer program, and were communicated with the goal of possible support for graduate school applications.

*Assessment Measures.* To assess effectiveness of the entire summer experience, the authors modified and replicated the methods of Kardash (2000), who evaluated the extent to which 14 research skills were enhanced by undergraduates' participation in NSF Research Experience for Undergraduates programs in natural and physical sciences. Kardash's participants self-rated their ability to perform the skills at the beginning and the end of the program using a 1-5 Likert scale survey (e.g. *To what extent do you feel you can understand contemporary concepts in your field?*). She found that interns' ratings were only modestly higher at the end of the program relative to the beginning. She discussed the possibility of lowering intern expectations prior to such experiences.

Noting that the phrase "in your field" in the original Kardash study items may be overly broad and mask positive outcomes situated in the specific research topic area, the Kardash survey was modified by expanding each item into three separate items, each tapping a different level of content: general psychology, applied psychology, and the specific research project area. For example, each student was asked—*to what extent do you feel you can understand contemporary concepts in the field of psychology, or in applied psychology, or in the area of research you are working on in this program?*

Each of the 12 interns responded to the three versions of the items at the beginning and then at the end of the program. At the beginning of the program, the items tapped ability and expectation (i.e. *to what extent do you feel you can? ...and to what extent do you feel the internship will help you?*) and at the end they tapped ability and attribution (i.e. *to what extent do you feel you can? ... and to what extent do you feel the internship did help you?*).

*Assessment Results.* At the beginning of the program, students rated their abilities significantly lower in the specific research area relative to the field of applied or general psychology. Students expected the internship would help them in all three domains, with greater gains in the specific project area.

After the program, students rated their abilities higher in the specific project domain. There were no significant increases in applied or general psychology domains. This increase in project specific knowledge may be the result of the effectiveness of the summer program in combination with the e-portfolio construction. Indeed, students' attributions at the end of the program suggest that both were effective in helping with skill acquisition and student sense of capability.

Faculty also rated their interns several weeks after the end of the program. Immediately prior to the ratings, faculty reviewed their intern's e-portfolio. Importantly, the faculty evaluations of student achievement (they were asked to respond only to items tapping "the area of research the student was working on") were in qualitative agreement with the student interns' ratings. This observation is consistent with the possibility that the e-portfolio was an effective basis for assessment of program effectiveness.

It is noteworthy that the summer program assessment reveals better improvements than those that Kardash (2000) reported. Perhaps this particular summer program was more effective overall, or perhaps the act of separating the assessment into three domains improved sensitivity. Possibly the e-portfolio enhanced both student and faculty awareness of increased capability. Although the assessment design does not permit separating the above possibilities, the results are consistent with the notion that e-portfolios may reveal achievement of undergraduate research learning goals and outcomes both to the student, as well as to those who may wish to assess the student.

## CONCLUSIONS

Technology can apparently assist development of practical, pedagogically-sound techniques for broad-based educational learning goals and outcomes. It may also permit practical embedded assessment that serves students, faculty, the academic community and external stakeholders.

The versatility of reflective e-portfolios as an effective learning and assessment technique is illustrated by the ease of adaptation in a discipline (psychology) whose style is somewhat removed from disciplines historically associated with portfolios (e.g. art, architecture, and education). Indeed, versatility of e-portfolios appears common across the Intro Lab, Methods courses, Senior Lab and summer undergraduate research programs.

Looking forward in science education, this versatility in reflective e-portfolio may prove helpful in support of new educational initiatives that involve integrated learning pedagogy. Considering the emerging national trend to include more undergraduates in faculty research, it is likely that e-portfolios can provide an effective pedagogy for enhancing and documenting the values embedded in such programs.

## REFERENCES

American Psychological Association. (2003). *The assessment cyberguide for learning goals and outcomes.* Washington, DC: Author. Retrieved November 1, 2004 from http://www.apa.org/ed/guidehomepage.html.

Berg, R. M., & Nasr, K. J. (2002). Achieving those difficult ABET Program educational outcomes through a capstone design course. *Proceedings of the 2002 American Society for Engineering Education Annual Conference and Exposition.*

Boyer Commission on Educating Undergraduates in the Research University. (1998). *Reinventing undergraduate education: A blueprint for America's research Universities.* Retrieved November 1, 2004 from http://notes.cc.sunysb.edu/Pres/boyer.nsf.

Brown, A., Campione, J., Webber, L., & McGilley, K. (1992). Interactive learning environments: A new look at assessment and instruction. In B. Gifford & M. O'Conner (Eds.), *Changing assessments: Alternative views of aptitude, achievement, and instruction* (pp. 121-211). Boston: Kluwer.

Garcia, C. E., & Clausen, E. C. (2000). Student portfolios–assessing criteria 2000. *Proceedings of the 2000 American Society for Engineering Education Annual Conference and Exposition.*

Gardner, H. (1992). Assessment in context: The alternative to standardized testing. In B. Gifford & M. O'Conner (Eds.), *Changing assessments: Alternative views of aptitude, achievement, and instruction* (pp. 77-119), Boston: Kluwer.

Huber, M. T., & Hutchings, P. (2004). *Integrative learning: mapping the terrain.* Retrieved November 1, 2004 from www.cargegiefoundation.org/LiberalEducation/appingTerrain.pdf.

Kardash, C. M. (2000). Evaluations of an undergraduate research experience: Perceptions of undergraduate interns and their faculty mentors. *Journal of Educational Psychology, 92*(1), 191-201.

Kwiatkowski, R. (2003). Trends in organizations and selection: An introduction. *Journal of Managerial Psychology, 18*(5), 382-394.

National Science Foundation. (1996). *Shaping the future: New expectations for undergraduate education in science, mathematics, engineering, and technology* (NSF Publication No. 96-139). Arlington, VA: Author.

Olds, B. M., & Pavelich, M. J. (1996) A portfolio-based assessment program. *Proceedings of the 1996 American Society for Engineering Education Annual Conference and Exposition.*

Panitz, B. (1998). Student E-portfolios. In Huband, F. L. (Ed.), *How do you measure success? Designing effective processes for assessing engineering education,* (pp 49-64). Washington, D.C.: American Society for Engineering Education.

Pigott, R., & Karr, B. (2001). Are we doing what we claim?: A e-portfolio approach to program performance assessment. *Proceedings of the 2001 American Society for Engineering Education Annual Conference and Exposition.*

Shavelson, R J., & Huang, L. (2003, January/February). Responding responsibly to the frenzy to assess learning in higher education. *Change,* 11-19.

Stephens, B. R. (in press). Laptops in psychology improve organization, e-portfolios, research laboratories, and writing laboratories. In L. Neilson & B. Weaver (Eds.). *New directions for teaching and learning, special issue: Enhancing learning using laptops in the classroom.* Jossey-Bass: San Francisco.

Stephens B. R., & Moore D. (2004). *A student self-report assessment survey for psychology program evaluation.* Manuscript submitted for publication.

Vygotsky, L. (1978). *Mind in society.* Cambridge: Harvard University Press.

Yancey, K. (1998). *Reflection in the writing classroom.* Logan: Utah State University Press.

Yancey, K. (2001). Student digital portfolios. In B. Cambridge (Ed.), *Electronic portfolios: Emerging practices in student, faculty and institutional learning.* Washington, D. C.: American Association of Higher Education.

Yancey, K., & Weiser, I. (1997) Situation portfolios: An introduction. In K. Yancey & I. Weiser (Eds.), *Situation e-portfolios: Four perspectives* (pp. 1-20). Logan: Utah State University Press.

**Note.** This chapter was based in part upon work supported by the National Science Foundation under Grant No. SES-0353698. Any opinions, findings and conclusions or recommendations expressed in this material are those of the authors, and do not necessarily reflect the views of the National Science Foundation. We are indebted to DeWayne Moore, Jan Murdoch, Kathleen Yancey, and Flora Riley for supportive suggestions that improved the pedagogical and technological innovations in our undergraduate programs.

# LEARNING A LA MODE DE PARIS

## Katherine Watson
### *Coastline Community College*

## INTRODUCTION

The relationship between culture-imbued teaching style and students' preferred modes of learning has been analyzed from an educator's point of view (Merrifield, 1996) as well as from a popular perspective (Rochefort, 2004). The Weltanschauung inherent in most francophone societies has been discussed in Baudry (2004), along with the French penchant for incorporating, or even imposing, worldview upon students. Consequences of an intimate relationship between culturally-based learning style preferences and traditional teaching modes and expectations are set forth in Ariza, Lapp, Rhone & Robinson (2003). In addition, the utility of new technologies to enhance language learning through varying teaching styles and founded in diverse cultures is discussed in Oxford, Rivera-Castillo, Feyten & Nutta. (2001).

## DESCRIPTION OF THE STUDY

Twelve adult students of French as a foreign language were studied over a period of twelve years to determine whether/how their learning style preferences changed as they worked in a completely online francophone course in reading, writing, and cultural awareness. Students self-selected themselves as Francophiles who had been exposed to traditional learning experiences in French: all students had traveled to at least one francophone area, and all had taken the equivalent of at least one year of college-level French. For the purposes of the study, they remained continuously enrolled for twelve years in an online course designed according to logic-and-analysis-based teaching and learning standards of francophone countries. That is, most of their work required reading, independent study, and research, reported upon in e-mail and in essays; no specific "due dates" were given beyond the end date of each term. Students consulted at least four times per semester with their instructor via e-mail; electronic bulletin board postings and twice-weekly live chat facilitated student-student as well as student-instructor discussion.

The study involved initial and semester analyses of learning style preferences throughout the twelve years. These analyses included holistic scoring of written essay assignments, timed records of work on objective tests, word-count and linguistic complexity analysis of open-ended answers to questions and collection of subjective comments.

Learning styles were initially analyzed in a gross, Kolb-style format, as summarized in Felder (1996). Each student was also given a Myers-Briggs (Myers & McCaulley, 1985) battery and presented with the Herrmann Brain Dominance Instrument (Hermann International, 1989) as it related to French-versus-American educational emphasis. Results from cross-cultural application of the Felder-Silverman Learning Style Model (Felder & Silverman, 1988) were shown to students to demonstrate the general francophone educational tendency to skew schoolwork toward the verbal, intuitive, inductive, and reflective, almost to the exclusion of the sensing, visual, active, and deductive.

Holistic analysis of essays written in French followed patterns used by the American Council on the Teaching of Foreign Languages (2001), the University of California, and by the Educational Testing Service for

English as a Second Language, English composition, and French as a Second Language. Scores ranged from 1 to 6 and reflected vocabulary and syntactic sophistication, rhetorical skill and level of abstraction.

Objective tests were done exclusively online; test software allowed for timing. These instruments were used to determine students' understanding of vocabulary and grammatical rules as well as their ability to identify main ideas and make inferences from short readings. Open-ended answers to questions were analyzed according to semantics and syntax, familiar or repeated word use, utterance length, and sentence complexity.

## FINDINGS

All twelve students completed the twelve years of the study and progressed in their abilities to understand and express themselves in French. All students advanced at least one level in American Council on the Teaching of Foreign Languages reading and writing proficiencies. Average sentence length in essays and in open-ended answers to questions changed from nine words at the beginning of the study to fourteen words at the end. Complex sentences outnumbered simple ones by two to one at the end, while they counted for only one third of the total at the beginning. A preference for abstract, inductive presentation using abstract words developed after each student had written only three essays.

All students achieved at least a score of 4 on all essays before the twelve years were completed, and six of the students received no scores below five during the last three years. Initial scores had ranged from 2 to 5, with only two students achieving 5 at the outset.

The four students initially Kolb-categorized as "concrete, active creative problem-solvers" were able to accommodate inductively-presented material after three semesters. Before the end of their second year of study they were able to argue their ideas inductively during live chat, as well as in their essays.

The three who were categorized as "concrete reflectives" began with questions about why they should be studying French from a French perspective. They ended by becoming more "abstract" in the Kolb classification, preferring organization, logic, and time for reflection, as is common among French learners.

The three who were initially classed as "abstract, active" learners retained their preference for the abstract but became less concerned about failure as their studies progressed. At the beginning of the study, these students were disquieted by a course requiring them to do work as they wished and with no due dates, but after only two semesters, they expressed satisfaction with that system, changing their learning style preference to the "reflective".

The two students initially classed as "concrete, active" began with the idea that they would be able to apply everything they learned to new, concrete situations to solve problems. After less than two years, they were seeking basic information about people and ideas for their own sake, placing things into new contexts with multidisciplinary perspectives. They began receiving 5 and 6 on their essay writing, in accordance with francophone school expectations.

## CONCLUSIONS AND RECOMMENDATIONS

Although it is clear that all twelve students in the current study progressed admirably in their understanding of French culture and their skills with the French language, the mechanism of their success is less obvious. Since these students were self-selected and since online students tend to enjoy intrinsic motivation to learn (Diaz & Cartnall, 1999), it is possible that they were guaranteed success.

Moreover, it is generally understood that immersion in a language provides the best learning benefits (Lecocq, et al., 2002). The French course in the present study offered as much immersion as students might be able to enjoy outside a francophone country, with page layout, colors, sounds, and movement all provided by native French speakers, with French interfaces in e-mail and bulletin boards, and with francophone correspondents. These factors could very well have expedited learning.

An obvious recommendation deriving from these conclusions is that other language courses be offered in a similar manner and over time. Institutions tend all too often to limit student study of foreign languages, permitting them only a few years of work, although competence is rarely attained in fewer than half a dozen years, even in one's native tongue.

It is further recommended that schools profit more fully from the convenience and dynamism available in the L2 (second language) areas of cyberspace. As Oxford et al. (2001) have stated, technology contributes to the educational goals of increasing student interest and motivation and of creating flexibility for learning. The broad range of content that the twelve students in the present study chose to work with, as well as the varying activities they pursued, demonstrate satisfaction with technological flexibility. And flexibility in any educational environment leads to shared control, something commonly desired by adult students who have already learned how to learn; this leads in turn to achievement of learning competence, with problems solved step-by-step, analytically, and from multiple perspectives in varying contexts.

The six students who were able after only a single semester to accept intuitive leaps as part of their learning process were enjoying what Oxford (1993) has called a "movement toward expertise," an approximation of communicative competence probably deriving from easy access to the abundant authentic L2 data available online.

Further recommendations derive from other conclusions to be made from this study. That is, although it is remarkable that any group of students would be willing to remain involved in a longitudinal study of this nature, more reliable data would accrue from the work of at least thirty students, for statistical purposes. And although it may appear to be politically incorrect in the twenty-first century to attempt to imbue learners with a "new" or "foreign" mode of apprehending information, the present study has demonstrated that learning à la mode can offer a wealth of understanding that is truly the crème de la crème.

## REFERENCES

American Council on the Teaching of Foreign Languages. (2001). *ACTFL Revised proficiency guidelines.* Retrieved November, 2003 from http://www.actfl.org/index.cfm? Weburl=/public/articles/index.cfm?cat=28

Ariza, E., Lapp, S., Rhone, A., & Robison, S. (April, 2003). Coping with cultures in the classroom. *Proceedings of the Hawaii International Conference on Education*, Honolulu, HI.

Baudry, P. (2004). *Français et Américains: L'Autre rive.* Paris: Village Mondial.

Diaz, D. P., & Cartnal, R. B. (1999). Students' learning styles in two classes: Online distance learning and equivalent on-campus. *College Teaching 47*(4), 130-135

Felder, R. (1996). Matters of style. *ASEE Prism, 6*(4), 18-23.

Felder, R., & Silverman, L. (1988). *Felder-Silverman Learning Style Model.* Retrieved December, 2004 from http://chat.carleton.ca/~tblouin/Felder/felder%20silverman %20online%20questionnaire.htm.

Hermann International. (1989). *Herrmann Brain Dominance Instrument.* Lake Lure, NC: The Ned Hermann Group.

Lecocq, K., Mousty, P., Kolinsky, R., Goetry, V., Morais, J., & Alegria, J. (2002). *Evaluation de programmes d'immersion en communauté française: Une etude longitudinale.* Bruxelles : Université Libre de Bruxelles. Retrieved November, 2004 from http://www.enseignement. be/@librairie/documents/ressources/096/synthese/article_2 002.pdf

Merrifield (1966). *Examining the language learning strategies used by French adult learners.* Birmingham, England: Aston University, Language Studies Unit.

Myers, I. B., & McCaulley, M. H. (1985). *Manual: A guide to the development and use of the Myers-Briggs Type Indicator.* Palo Alto, CA: Consulting Psychologists Press.

Oxford, R. (1993). Intelligent computers for language learning. *Computer-Assisted Language Learning, 6*(2), 173-179.

Oxford, R., Rivera-Castillo, Y., Feyten, C., & Nutta, J. (2001). *Computers and more: Creative uses of technology for learning a second or foreign language.* INSA de Lyon. Retrieved November, 2004, from http://ltsc.ph-karlsruhe.de/Oxford.pdf

Rochefort, W. H. (2004). *Better understand France and the French.* Retrieved December, 2004 from www.understandingfrance.org/.

# CONTRIBUTORS

**Robert J. Beichner**
Alumni Distinguished
Undergraduate Professor, Physics
*North Carolina State University*
E-mail: beichner@ncsu.edu

**Julia Claxton**
Senior Lecturer, Management,
Community and Communication
*York St. John College, UK*
E-mail: J.Claxton@yorksj.ac.uk

**Joseph-Rene Corbeil**
Assistant Professor,
Curriculum & Instruction
*University of Texas at Brownsville*
and *Texas Southmost College*
E-mail: rcorbeil@UTB.edu

**David B. Dahlberg**
Associate Professor,
Business Administration
*College of St. Catherine*
E-mail: dbdahlberg@stkate.edu

**Jeana M. Davis**
Project Coordinator, Learning Technologies
and Professional Development
*Florida Community College at Jacksonville*
E-mail: jmdavis@fccj.edu

**Gregory B. DiNovis**
Assistant Professor,
Business Administration
*College of St. Catherine*
E-mail:  gbdinovis@stkate.edu

**Ruby Evans**
Associate Professor
and Program Coordinator,
Educational Research,
Technology and Leadership
*University of Central Florida*
E-mail: revans@mail.ucf.edu

**Barclay Hudson**
Faculty, Masters Program
in Organizational Development
*Fielding Graduate Institute*
E-mail: bhudson@fielding.edu

**Yanick Rice Lamb**
Lecturer/News-Editorial
Sequence Coordinator
*Howard University*
yrlamb@aol.com

**Cheng-Chang Pan**
Assistant Professor,
Curriculum & Instruction
*University of Texas at Brownsville*
and *Texas Southmost College*
E-mail: sampan@utb.edu

**Claire Rundle**
Assistant Director
for Faculty Development
*Regent University*
clairun@regent.edu

**Jeffery M. Saul**
Assistant Professor, Physics
*University of Central Florida*
E-mail: saul@physics.ucf.edu

**Nancy A. Stanlick**
Assistant Professor, Philosophy
*University of Central Florida*
E-mail: stanlick@mail.ucf.edu

**Benjamin R. Stephens**
Associate Professor and
Undergraduate Coordinator, Psychology
*Clemson University*
E-mail: bstephe@clemson.edu

**Michael J. Sullivan**
Assistant Professor,
Curriculum & Instruction
*University of Texas at Brownsville*
and *Texas Southmost College*
E-mail: msullivan@utb.edu

**Katherine Watson**
Professor, Distance Learning
*Coastline Community College*
E-mail: bizarrerie@aol.com

**Barbara E. Weaver**
Information Resource Consultant II
*Clemson University*
E-mail: weaver2@clemson.edu